DUDE, DON'T BE A LEMUEL

A TEENAGE GUIDE TO AVOIDING LEMUELITIS

DUDE, DON'T BE A LEMUEL

A TEENAGE GUIDE TO AVOIDING LEMUELITIS

DAVID BOWMAN

ISBN 13: 978-1-59955-943-8

LIBRARY OF CONGRESS CATALOGING-IN-PUBLICATION DATA
Bowman, David, 1974- author.
Dude! don't be a Lemuel! / David Bowman.
p. cm.
Summary: A humorous look at the Book of Mormon characters Laman and Lemuel.
ISBN 978-1-59955-943-8
1. Lemuel (Book of Mormon figure) 2. Laman (Book of Mormon figure) 3. Nephi (Book of Mormon figure) 4. Christian life--Mormon authors. I. Title.
BX8627.3.B69 2011
289.3'22--dc23

2011017420

Printed in the United States of America

10 9 8 7 6 5 4 3 2 1

Contents

Before we get started . . .

Laman & Lemuel.

Two classic characters from the Book of Mormon. Just hearing their names brings to mind a whole list of not-so-complimentary adjectives ("dumb and dumber" comes to mind for me). Once, at a youth conference I was speaking at, I even met a young man whose parents had named him Laman. True story. Yeah, I know . . . What were his parents *thinking*? ☺

Yes, good ol' Lemon and Lamo . . . what an interesting pair of knuckleheads. You're familiar with their story. Reading the first sixty-five or so pages of the Book of Mormon, you might have asked yourself, "*Dude*, what is their *problem*?"

You've probably been amazed at how these two brothers could so completely "miss the boat" throughout their journey to the Promised Land . . . despite seeing angels, experiencing miracles, and even hearing the voice of the Lord.

Yes, it's easy to give them a bad rap. BUT were L&L completely "bad"?

> *Didn't they leave Jerusalem with their father, as commanded by the Lord?*
>
> *Didn't they go back to get the brass plates, as commanded by the Lord (Laman even going in by himself the first time to talk to Laban)?*
>
> *Didn't they journey through the wilderness, as commanded by the Lord?*
>
> *Didn't they help Nephi build a ship, as commanded by the Lord?*
>
> *And didn't they sail to and settle in the Promised Land, as commanded by the Lord?*

AND . . . here's a long list of positive things Nephi mentioned about them along the way:

> "[L&L] did soften their hearts"—1 Nephi 7:19
>
> "[L&L did] pray unto the Lord their God for forgiveness"—1 Nephi 7:21
>
> "[L&L] did give thanks unto the Lord their God"—1 Nephi 7:22
>
> "[L&L] did humble themselves before the Lord"—1 Nephi 16:5
>
> "[L&L] did humble themselves before the Lord, and did give thanks unto him"—1 Nephi 16:32
>
> "[L&L] did turn away their anger, and did repent of their sins"—1 Nephi 16:39
>
> "[L&L] said: We know of a surety that the Lord is with thee [Nephi]"—1 Nephi 17:55
>
> "[L&L] did worship the Lord, and did go forth with me [Nephi]"—1 Nephi 18:1
>
> "[L&L] did humble themselves again before the Lord"—1 Nephi 18:4

So, if Laman & Lemuel weren't *entirely* "wicked," then what is it about this Less-than-Dynamic Duo that we find so troubling? Why did they bring such anxiety and sorrow to their parents and to Nephi? What was it about them that displeased the Lord?

Simple. They had Lemuelitis.

> **Lemuelitis**, as defined by wikidpedia: (noun) A most yucky disease! Very widespread. Difficult to detect. Often misdiagnosed. Highly contagious. No one is immune. Affected persons display a variety of symptoms, making

> them most grouchy and unattractive. If not treated, Lemuelitis will continue to fester until it becomes fatal (spiritually). Found in all age groups, but especially prevalent among teenagers.

"So," you might be asking, "what *are* these symptoms? Do *I* have Lemuelitis? If so, is there a cure? How do I treat it? If I don't have it, how do I avoid it? I'm scared. I don't want to become unattractive. ☹ I need answers, doc!!"

Well, my friend, who better to learn these answers from than Mr. Lemuelitis *himself.* In this book, you'll see firsthand the effects of this dreaded disease and how someone with Lemuelitis (that would be Lemuel) views the world.

And how do you treat it, you ask? Well, if Lemuelitis is the disease, then Nephibuprofen is the cure!

We'll take a closer look at this stalwart younger brother to see what he does to fight off infection. ☺

Now, before we start, I need you to get a Book of Mormon. I will refer to things that you will want to read straight from Nephi's account. Also, at the beginning of each chapter of this book, I will give you the reference to where you can read the same story (from

Nephi's perspective) in your Book of Mormon. If you read those references *first*, they'll be fresh on your mind and you'll get a lot more out of this book. If that's "too hard" or sounds like "too much work", then, uh . . . what's that I smell? . . . >*sniff*< . . . >*sniff*< . . . Eeww, is that Lemuelitis I smell floating around in the air? Uh-oh! You better keep reading!

All right, you ready? Great! Let's take a closer look at this well-known story, but from a little different perspective . . .

Hhhmmm...

THE BOOK OF
LEMUEL
(LAMAN
KEEP OUT!)

Chapter 1

Uh, Dad? You Can't be Serious.

(Nephi's version—1 Nephi 2)
(Remember! Read Nephi's version first, and then keep reading here)

I, Lemuel, having been born of wacky parents (well, mainly my dad), therefore I was forced to leave the land of my inheritance, and my gold, and my buddies, and my souped-up four-wheel drive chariot, to perish in the wilderness, therefore I make a record of my proceedings in my days.

Yea, I make a record in the language of my frustration, having been afflicted with all manner of raw deals in the course of my days.

For it came to pass that my father, Lehi, went among the good people of Jerusalem, declaring unto them all manner of **BIZARRE** rantings and ravings concerning wickedness and destruction; yea, completely embarrassing me, insomuch that multitudes of my friends spake unto me, saying: **Dude, what's up with your dad?**

NOW THESE THINGS HE SPAKE UNTO THEM BECAUSE OF A DREAM HE HAD, AND THUS WE SEE THE EFFECTS OF ONE TOO MANY PIECES OF UNLEAVENED BREAD PARTAKEN OF BEFORE GOING TO BED.

AND IT CAME TO PASS THAT MY FATHER SPAKE UNTO US, SAYING: **Behold, I have dreamed a dream, in the which the Lord hath commanded us to leave all of our possessions and depart into the wilderness.**

AND MY BROTHER LAMAN SPAKE UNTO HIM, SAYING: **WHAT!!!???!!??**

DO YE SUPPOSE THAT I CAN LEAVE MY SPOT AS STARTING QUARTERBACK OF THE JERUSALEM COMMUNITY COLLEGE FOOTBALL TEAM? YEA, DO YE SUPPOSE THAT I CAN LEAVE MY EXCEEDINGLY FAIR CHEERLEADER GIRLFRIEND? BEHOLD, I SAY UNTO YOU, NAY.

AND AFTER THIS MANNER DID WE WEEP AND WAIL AND GNASH OUR TEETH.

NEVERTHELESS, OUR YOUNGEST BROTHER, NEPHI, WHO IS EXCEEDINGLY ANNOYING AND HIGHLY FAVORED OF OUR FATHER, DID KISS UP EXCEEDINGLY AND DID CHEERFULLY SUBMIT TO THIS IMPROMPTU, INDEFINITE CAMPING TRIP.

AND IT CAME TO PASS THAT OUR WHINING AND PLEADING WAS TO NO AVAIL, FOR IT SUFFICETH ME TO SAY THAT THIS WAS SOMETHING WE WEREN'T GOING TO GET OUT OF. AND THUS ENDED THE COMMENCEMENT OF . . . MY LIFE.

WHAT'S **REALLY** HAPPENING HERE

As we start the story, it's really all about **vision**.

Nephi has it. Laman and Lemuel don't. Let's talk about it:

Nephi has "great desires to know the mysteries of God" (1 Nephi 2:16). He sees the bigger picture. He's not focused on the negative aspects of leaving his current lifestyle or the hardships of wilderness survival. He's focused on the *real purpose* in leaving Jerusalem—that is, to be led to a *much greater* Land of Promise. Nephi's sights are set on the end goal.

In other words, Nephi has **caught the vision:**

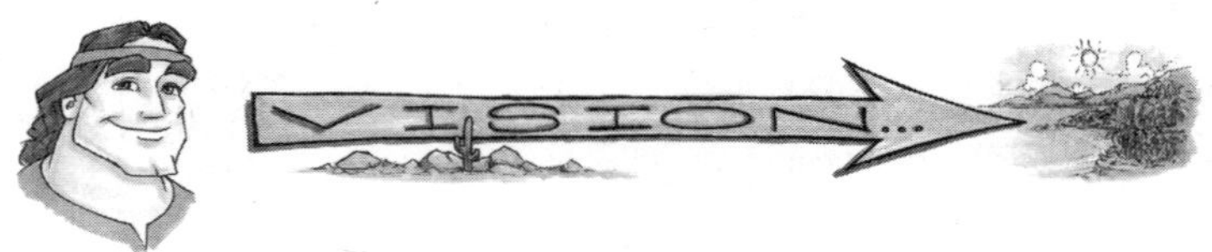

Laman & Lemuel, on the other hand, have zero desires to know the mysteries of God. They don't turn to the Lord to try to find some bigger meaning in it all. L&L couldn't care less! All they see is everything they are leaving behind and that it's so NOT FAIR! Without the vision of *why* they are leaving their hometown for a life in the wilderness, L&L are nothing but frustrated. No wonder they're so grouchy.

Laman's & Lemuel's vision looks something like this:

The Promised Land? Or the rear end of the camel in front of you? It's all about the extent of your vision.

DUDE! DON'T BE A LEMUEL

Now, read 1 Nephi 2:11–12 closely and see if you can find the reason for L&L's murmuring:

> Is it the fact that they have to leave behind all their stuff? (v. 11)
>
> Is it because they hate camping? (v. 11)
>
> Is it because they're sure Dad has gone off his rocker? (v. 11)

At first glance, you might think these complaints are the issue. But does it go deeper than that?

I believe the real reason for their bad attitudes is found in this phrase: "(Laman & Lemuel) knew not the dealings of that God who had created them" (v. 12).

> Failing to understand the 'dealings' of the Lord with His children—meaning His relations with and treatment of His children—is very fundamental. Murmuring is but one of the symptoms.
>
> (Elder Neal A. Maxwell, "Lessons from Laman and Lemuel," *Ensign*, Nov. 1999)

Not knowing your Heavenly Father is at the heart of Lemuelitis. It's the root of the disease. And without this knowledge of how God works with His children, one will always resent any sacrifices he/she has to make for God. As Elder Maxwell states, murmuring and complaining are just **symptoms** of Lemuelitis . . . the same way aches, congestion, and a fever are symptoms of the flu. Does that make sense?

And the sad thing is . . . L&L never TRY to grow closer to their Heavenly Father and learn His purposes. Throughout their entire journey to the Promised Land, they remain apathetic (unless they're about to be killed, *then* they care!). You'd think *something* would get through to these guys. Nope, not so much. Dude, don't be a Lemuel!

NEPHI'S QUOTABLE QUOTE

And it came to pass that I, Nephi, being exceedingly young, nevertheless being large in stature, and also having great desires to know of the mysteries of God, wherefore, I did cry unto the Lord; and behold he did visit me, and did soften my heart that I did believe all the words which had been spoken by my father; wherefore, I did not rebel against him like unto my brothers. (1 Nephi 2:16)

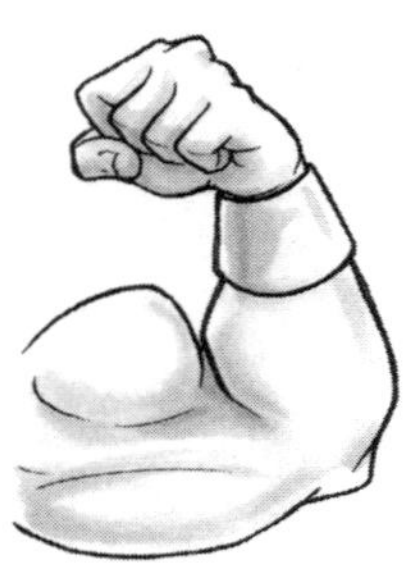

(By the way, don't you just love how Nephi threw in the part about his large in stature-ness, just to remind us how buff he was, even though it has nothing to do with the rest of the verse. 😊)

Let's take a closer look at Nephi's Quotable Quote for clues as to *HOW* Nephi caught the vision:

Nephi is young . . . check. Nephi is buff . . . got it. Moving on . . .

HOW 'BOUT THAT NEPHI

Nephi has "great desires to know the mysteries of God." Crucial point! You gotta want it! The Lord can't work with you until you actually put forth some effort on your own.

Next, Nephi "did cry unto the Lord." Key word here is "cry." Nephi doesn't just routinely go through the motions, saying the standard prayer phrases. He reaches deep into his soul and sincerely talks with his Father in Heaven.

Then, because of his efforts, Nephi describes how the Lord "did visit me, and **did soften my heart** that I did believe all the words which had been spoken by my father." Whoa! Time out! Did you catch the part about the Lord softening Nephi's heart?? (You better have, because I **bolded** and underlined it for you. ☺) You mean Nephi, at first, might have had a hard time with all this *too*? *His* heart needed softening? He wasn't Mr. Go-and-Do right off the bat . . . but actually might have been questioning his father a little? In other words, you mean Nephi was normal?

That's what I love about Nephi. He wasn't born with spiritual super powers like we sometimes imagine.

He isn't perfect. Nephi is simply a good kid who *wants* to grow closer to the Lord and be better than he is. And the Lord responds to Nephi's desires.

HOWEVER, does Nephi have the vision yet of **WHY** they have to leave Jerusalem and where they are going? No. The Lord simply softens his heart so Nephi will believe his dad. (At this point, Nephi's record doesn't mention Lehi actually telling his family about going to a Promised Land . . . just that the Lord commanded them to depart into the wilderness).

It isn't until verse 20, after continued faith and diligence and "crying unto the Lord," that Nephi is rewarded with the knowledge that they are being "led to a land of promise; yea, even a land which I have prepared for you; yea, a land which is choice above all other lands." That's when he gains the vision for himself!

THAT WAS **THEN** THIS IS **NOW**

One thing as we start:

Nephi did "liken all scriptures unto us, that it might be for our profit and learning" (1 Nephi 19:23). We want to do the same thing. So, I need you to keep the following analogy fresh in your mind as you read this book:

Lehi and his family's journey to the Promised Land
= (is a parallel of)
Your journey through life toward eventual exaltation

Read those words to yourself again. Okay, read 'em again. Now three more times. Got it stuck there? Cemented in your brain? Great!

My young friend, you are just beginning your journey, so to speak. Which means right now (the teenage years) is critical! You have the path to *your* promised land (eternal life) laid out before you. It's an awesome, exciting adventure! The rewards are huge! But it's up to you to get on the path.

Now, your journey is **not** going to be easy. It wasn't supposed to be easy (so no whining ☺). As a member of Christ's restored church, with the celestial kingdom as your end goal, a lot will be asked of you. That's why the only way to succeed in this journey is to **catch the vision.**

What do I mean by "catching the vision"?

In my experience, catching the vision is when the gospel starts to **feel real** to you. You start living the gospel because you WANT to . . . not because your parents want you to or because you're "supposed to." You have sought after the Lord for yourself—on your own—and have felt the Holy Ghost witness to you that it's all true. You have gained a conviction of who you really are, why you are here on Earth, who Jesus Christ is, and what you can become through His power. The Great Plan of Happiness becomes your plan. That's the vision!

Have you caught the vision? Do you see Heavenly Father's bigger picture for your life? Do you *want* to?

Then follow in the footsteps of our man, Nephi. Remember, it's not just **what** he did, but **how** he did it that makes the difference. He turned to the Lord *like he meant it.* Nobody had to keep telling him what he was supposed to do. He reached out to his Father in Heaven with the same focus some of you young men have when playing your favorite video game. Whoa, now *that's* focus!

I remember the first time I felt like I caught the vision. I was fourteen years old at my first Especially For Youth conference. I wasn't a "bad" kid, but I just didn't feel like I had much of a testimony. I felt kinda empty inside. I prayed sincerely those first couple of nights (probably my first time ever praying like that) asking Father to help me feel . . . something. I wasn't sure exactly what . . . just to feel that He was there, I guess.

There was a testimony meeting near the end of the conference. For the first time in my life I listened intently to everyone getting up. I was focused. I was "in the zone," you might say.

And then it hit me—a sudden feeling whooshing over me. It's hard to describe. It was kind of like this amazing realization that all the stuff that I'd been taught since I was a Sunbeam, all the gospel truths I'd grown up with and not really appreciated, they were actually *true*!! It was all truth! It wasn't just a bunch of stories that the adults made up and told us so that we would be good kids. Heavenly Father was real, and He loved me. Jesus Christ was real and actually died for me. Joseph Smith was real and actually saw God and Jesus like he claimed he did. It was all real! I was awestruck!

It's hard to put into words the feeling I had that night, but it was real. I knew that Heavenly Father had answered my prayer because of my "great desires" to feel His love. I felt like I had caught the vision that night, and it was the best feeling in the world.

BY THE WAY

Please remember that.

Catching the vision is a gift from God. Heavenly Father *blesses you* with vision. He gives it to you, through the Holy Ghost, in His own time and in His own way. So don't get discouraged if your prayers aren't answered instantly. Part of the test is if you'll keep at it with the "great desires" of a Nephi.

Many young people catch the vision slowly, little by little. It doesn't have to be one big "Aha!" spiritual experience. Several small, quiet moments of vision-catching have the same effect as one big one.

Catching the vision is <u>not</u> a once-in-a-lifetime experience. The vision needs to be recaptured again and again, over and over, all throughout your life. Constant effort is needed. We'll talk more about that as we continue the journey.

SUMMING IT UP

Doctor's Report

℞

Disease LEMUELITIS as shown by . . .
"Not knowing the dealings of that God who has created you"
(1 Nephi 2:12)

Symptoms
- Focusing your attention on worldly things
- Complaining about having to give up those things for God
- Eventually obeying but with a bad attitude

Prescription Catch the vision & see the BIGGER picture

Dr. Bowman

Signature

YOUR DOSAGE OF SCRIPTURE POWER

JOHN 17:3

REFILL AS OFTEN AS NEEDED

CHAPTER 2

GETTING THE PLATES OF BRASS . . .
. . . WHAT AN IMPOSSIBLE TASK!

(Nephi's version—1 Nephi 3–4)

AND IT CAME TO PASS THAT AFTER WE HAD TRAVELED FOR THE SPACE OF THREE DAYS IN THE WILDERNESS, WE PITCHED OUR TENTS IN SOME RANDOM VALLEY BY THE SHORES OF THE RED SEA.

AND MY FATHER SPAKE UNTO ME, LEMUEL, SAYING: **O that thou mightest be like unto this valley, firm and dead last and immovable in . . . uh . . . umm . . . something**. BLAH, BLAH, BLAH-ETH. NEVERTHELESS, I AM HIGHLY FAVORED OVER MY OLDER BROTHER, LAMAN. FOR BEHOLD, FATHER HATH ONLY NAMED A RIVER AFTER HIM. YEA, I HATH THE **ENTIRE VALLEY** (WHICH IS EXCEEDINGLY LARGER IN STATURE) NAMED AFTER ME. HA!

And it came to pass that my father spake unto us saying: **Behold, the Lord hath commanded you to return to Jerusalem, to the house of Laban, to obtain the plates of brass.** And I spake unto myself saying: **Surely this would have been nice to know BEFORE we left Jerusalem!**

And Laman and I did labor diligently to persuade our father to get real, saying: **This is a hard thing which ye have required of us, and behold, hard things are yucky.**

Nevertheless, Nephi, being exceedingly large in stature, did drag us back to the land of our inheritance. And as we went forth, he did sing an exceedingly annoying song; yea, something about "I will go, I will do."

Behold, it came to pass that Laman went forth alone to the house of Laban to obtain the plates of brass.

(What if they could text back then?)

TEXTING

Lemuel: R U there yet?
Laman: yes. Im talking to him right now. GtG
Lemuel: GL

Time passes . . .

Laman: IB. Failure.
Lemuel: LOL WTG
Laman: SH^!! QL
Lemuel: W/E

And behold, Laman did fail miserably.

Thus, we did gather together our gold, and our silver-coated game system, and the deed to our cabin on Mount Hermon, to trade with Laban for the plates of brass.

And it came to pass that when Laban saw our property, and that it was exceedingly great, he did lust after it, and did send his servants to slay us, that he might obtain our riches, therefore, we did hustle it out of there, yea, even with a great hustle.

Wherefore, having lost all our stuff, Laman and I did commence to smite Nephi with a rod, for behold, we hath decided that everything is his fault. And we did also smite Sam, our other younger brother, because he doth listen to Nephi.

And it came to pass that some time previous to the smiting, behold, Nephi did persuade one of his friends to gird himself in the garments of an angel and to hide himself within the rocks. And now, behold, as we were smiting Nephi and Sam, his friend did pop out and stand before us, and he spake unto us, saying: **Why do you smite your younger brother with a rod?** Nevertheless, I, Lemuel, being exceedingly **LARGE IN SMARTNESS,** knew that he was not a real angel.

And it came to pass that after the "angel" had departed, behold, my brother Nephi did continue to be annoying; yea, he did speak unto us of being strong like unto Moses and of God delivering Laban into our hands (blah, blah, blah-eth). Now when he had thus spoken these words, we did decide to try one more time, insomuch that Nephi did finally shut up, which was according to our desire.

And now, behold, I, Lemuel, having hid myself without the walls (that's a fancy way of saying outside of the walls), with my eldest brother, Laman, and my other goody-goody brother Sam,

DO TARRY HERE FOR THE SPACE OF MANY HOURS WHILE NEPHI HATH GONE FORTH ALONE TO OBTAIN THE PLATES OF BRASS. YEA, MY LOINS DOTH HURT FROM SITTING UPON THIS ROCK, WHICH IS EXCEEDING HARD, AND GREAT IS THE SORENESS THEREOF.

TEXTING

Laman: This TS (totally stinks)
Lemuel: Yea. Hey---whats that noise??
Laman: IHNI. WAS . . . DUDE! Its LABAN!! ☹
Lemuel: ☹!

AND IT CAME TO PASS THAT IT WASN'T LABAN AFTER ALL, BUT NEPHI GIRDING HIMSELF IN THE GARMENTS OF LABAN. YEA, HE DID FRIGHTEN THE BA-JEE-BEES OUT OF US. HA HA, VERY FUNNY, NEPHI! AND HE DID LUCK OUT IN ALL THINGS, INSOMUCH THAT HE DID SOMEHOW OBTAIN THE PLATES OF BRASS, THEREFORE THE FIVE OF US (VERILY, I SAY FIVE BECAUSE NEPHI HATH DUPED SOME POOR SAP NAMED ZORAM INTO JOINING US) DID RETURN TO THE TENT OF OUR FATHER.

WHAT'S **REALLY** HAPPENING HERE

Well, sons of Lehi, here's the first real test of your vision: *a seemingly impossible task given to you from the Lord*. How are you going to respond?? Howz your faith-o-meter??

Nephi . . . You totally ROCK!

Laman & Lemuel . . . You totally BONK!

This story is where Nephi puts into **action** the vision he so recently obtained. In his race of endurance to the Promised Land, Nephi is off to a great start, full of strength and vitality!

L&L? Well, they put into **action** their faithless whining about having to do something "hard." In their race of endurance to the Promised Land, L&L are stuck on the starting line, wondering, "Aww man! Do I *really* have to run this dumb race? My neck is stiff."

DUDE! DON'T BE A LEMUEL

Okay, Lemuel, so you're not as strong in your faith as your younger brother Nephi. But neither is your brother Sam. Yet Sam chooses to lean on the faith and example of Nephi, thus helping his own faith in the process. Who's example do you choose to follow, Lemuel?

"And it came to pass that Laman was angry with me, . . . and also was Lemuel, for he hearkened unto the words of Laman" (1 Nephi 3:28). You choose *Laman* as your example? Ah, Lemuel . . . you failed that test, brother!

Moral: Let's choose wisely which "friends" we hang with and allow to influence us. It's one of the biggest choices you'll make in your teenage years. Why? Because you *will* become who your friends are. Seriously. Trust me on this one.

"**KNEW NOT** THE DEALINGS OF THAT GOD WHO HAD CREATED THEM"

> Fundamental . . . was Laman and Lemuel's not understanding that a tutoring God may require difficult things of His children . . . Their sad expectation of ease was evident in their bristling over getting the plates from Laban, enduring the harsh wilderness, building a ship, and crossing a vast ocean. Dulled and desensitized, Laman and Lemuel simply didn't share Nephi's confidence that the Lord would never command His children to do difficult things, except the Lord first prepares the way.
>
> Elder Neal A. Maxwell, "Lessons from Laman and Lemuel," *Ensign*, Nov. 1999.)

L&L "knew not" that when God gives you a commandment that seems really hard or impossible, He doesn't leave you to do it alone. Loving Fathers don't do that to their children. They're intent on seeing their children succeed . . . *and* for them to experience the growth that comes through the process.

THAT WAS **THEN** THIS IS **NOW**

In your journey through life to your promised land, you are gonna come across this guy.

His name is Goliath. He doesn't like you. (Can you tell?) You're gonna have to face him—and perhaps face many Goliaths in your lifetime. Like defeating Goliath was for young David (1 Samuel 17), like getting the plates of brass was for Nephi . . . you too will have seemingly impossible tasks to tackle, trials to tread through, obstacles to overcome, and so on. Hey, don't be surprised by this. It's all part of Father's Plan that you signed up for in the premortal world.

The real trick is how you choose to respond to these challenges. Do they make you *bitter* . . . or do they make you *better*?

Now, let's take a look at some of the things Nephi does to conquer his Goliath. Although everyone's Goliaths are different, you can use these same "Nephibuprofen stones" when confronting your personal Goliath because the principles apply to any situation. (And yes, you will need your scriptures to look these up. Now, now, don't give me that Sunday School "Awww . . . you-mean-I-have-to-actually- pull-them-out-from-under-my-chair-and-unzip-them-and-use-them?" whine. 😊 Don't be Lemuel.)

Stone #1—1 Nephi 3:7 We all know and love this verse (as we should!). But where did Nephi get the motivation to make such a powerful statement? Did he just pull that kind of spiritual strength out of nowhere? Hhhhmmm . . . (hint: what was Nephi doing right *before* this???) Read vs. 1. Are you having constant, daily experiences with the Lord?

Stone #2—1 Nephi 3:15 Okay, so their first try didn't work. But just look at Nephi's sheer determination in this verse. Now that's Bounce-Back-itude! Instead of giving up, he makes a COVENANT with the Lord that they will not quit until they have succeeded. For Nephi, when the going gets tough . . . the tough gets its game on!

Stone #3—1 Nephi 3:16 Be resourceful! That means be creative, come up with solutions, look around you for things that could help. In other words, *use your <u>brain</u>* as well as your faith.

Stone #4—1 Nephi 3:29 You might not have an angel come down, but know that Heavenly Father is always there while you battle your Goliath. He does not abandon you!

Stone #5—1 Nephi 4:2 Have scriptural heroes! Nephi did. He saw Moses as a real person, someone he could strive to be like and expect similar results when he did.

Stone #6—1 Nephi 4:5 Ya got people bringin' ya down? Bein' a "bad influence"? Crampin' your ability to tune into the spirit? Then leave 'em, for heaven's sake! Go solo if you have to.

These are just a few strategies Nephi gives you for battling your personal Goliath. See if you can find more.

NEPHI'S QUOTABLE QUOTE

And I was led by the spirit, not knowing beforehand the things which I should do. (1 Nephi 4:6)

In essence, Nephi is saying, "Hey, I don't know how I'm gonna do it! But that's okay. 'Cause I know the Lord will guide me step by step until I have done it. And that's good enough for me." Wow. Now that's faith!

HOW 'BOUT THAT NEPHI

Does it ever bug you that the Lord commanded Nephi to *kill* Laban? I mean, isn't "Thou shalt not *kill*" one of the Ten Commandments? Couldn't Nephi have just taken Laban's clothes and gotten the brass plates *without* chopping Laban's head off? Why so harsh?

Well, here's a cool tidbit for ya:

The Ten Commandments are found in Exodus chapter 20. In Exodus chapter 21, the Lord continues to give His law to Moses. In verse 12, the Lord says: "He that smiteth a man, so that he die, shall be put to death." In other words, thou shalt not kill. Pretty straight forward.

BUT, in the next verse, the Lord gives this interesting exception to that commandment: "And if a man lie not in wait, but God deliver him into his hand; then I will appoint thee a place whither he shall flee." In other words, if it isn't pre-meditated murder ("lie not in wait"), and God "delivers" somebody into your hands, then the killing seems to be not only justified, but God will also show you a special place where you can run away to. Hmmmm.

So, while Nephi is psyching himself up to actually kill Laban (which Nephi does NOT want to do, by the way . . . yuck!), the Spirit reminds him THREE TIMES how the Lord has "**delivered him into thy hands**" (1 Nephi 4:11, 12, 17). Why does the Spirit keep using that specific phrase? Why is it so important? Do ya think Nephi could have been familiar with the verse in Exodus? Nephi had well-to-do parents who educated him and taught him the Mosaic Law.

I believe Nephi knew his scriptures. He knew that in this particular instance, according to the law, killing Laban would be allowed because the Lord had "delivered him into his hands." And afterwards, didn't the Lord appoint Nephi and his family a place whither they could flee to (aka: into the wilderness and later to the Promised Land), just as He promised?

Nephi was not going against the Lord's written commandments to kill Laban. He was actually doing exactly what the scriptures said he *should* do. Go Nephi!

BY THE WAY

Here's indisputable proof that the Book of Nephi was, indeed, written by a guy:

Nephi creeps into Jerusalem alone. He sees a drunken dude passed out. He gets closer. It's Laban! Wow! Imagine the odds! And what's the first thing he thinks after making this huge discovery? Perhaps, *"Oh, I wonder if he's all right"* or *"Thank you, Lord, for this blessing"*? No, no. In the next verse Nephi goes off about . . . how incredibly cool Laban's SWORD is!!

> And I beheld his sword, and I drew it forth from the sheath thereof; and the hilt thereof was of pure gold, and the workmanship thereof was exceedingly fine, and I saw that the blade thereof was of the most precious steel. (1 Nephi 4:9)

It's like he's thinkin', "Yeah, Laban might be passed out . . . but hey, check out his SWORD! It's awesome! Look at its hilt, and the blade . . . Wow, this baby is QUAL-I-TY!" Typical guy, into their boy toys. ☺

SUMMING IT UP

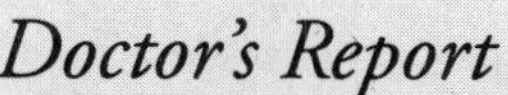

Disease LEMUELITIS as shown by . . .
"Lacking faith that you can do 'hard things' that the Lord commands"

Symptoms
- Whining about it.
- Giving up easily.
- Stiffneckedness

Prescription Take six Nephibuprofen stones and call me in the morning

Dr. Bowman

Signature

Chapter 3

Going Back to Get Our Hotties

(Nephi's version—1 Nephi 7)

And it came to pass that after only a few days, Father spake unto my brothers and I, saying: **Return again to Jerusalem and bring back Ishmael and his family, yea, and his many daughters, so that ye may take wives with you into the wilderness.**

And I spake unto myself, saying: **Now that's more like it!** And we did straightway return to the land of Jerusalem, happily singing with one accord, "I will go, I will do!"

And it came to pass that we went up unto the house of Ishmael, and behold, I, Lemuel, did gain favor in the sight of all his daughters, yea, having power over their hearts because of my EXCEEDING MANLINESS, insomuch that they did plead with their father to PLEEEAAASEE let them go with us into the wilderness. (Oh, and Nephi did speak something about the word of the Lord . . . blah, blah, blah-eth)

And after having obtained our hotties, we did journey again to the tent of our Father.

And while we were thus journeying, Laman spake unto our multitude, saying: **Behold, What are we doing-eth?! For behold, we still have lives back in Jerusalem as it were, and much riches and partyings doth await us there? Let us, therefore, return to the good life! What say ye?**

And Nephi did boldly stretch forth his goody-goody-ness, and spake many words unto us, encouraging us to be faithful unto the Lord, even unto the obtaining of a far BETTER land, yea, even a NEW LAND OF PROMISE! ☺

And I, Lemuel, did murmur unto myself saying: **Every party doth need a pooper, and thus, we inviteth you, Nephi.**

And it came to pass that Laman and I were angry with Nephi and did bind him with cords, that we might leave him in the wilderness to "bond" with nature for a season.

(What if they could Skype back then?)

Uh, well, he's . . . uh . . . kinda tied up right now. WAIT! No! I mean, he's . . . uh . . .

Well, when you see him, tell him these plates of brass are wonderful! What a blessing! I . . .

Your father won't stop reading them.
OK, Dad . . . will do. Gotta go.

And it came to pass that Nephi did somehow escape from the cords from which he was bound, yea, they were loosed from off his hands and feet, and Laman did cry unto me, saying: **O ye incompetent brother! How is it that ye have not learned to tie something stronger than a granny knot?!**

And as we sought to beat up Nephi, behold, the cutest of the daughters of Ishmael did plead with me to spare his life, insomuch that she did look up at me with her big brown eyes, and did hold my hand, and did start to cry, and did . . . did . . . ohhh . . . fine!

Furthermore, we did start to feel kinda bad for being so mean to Nephi (but don't telleth anyone), and did ask for his forgiveness, which he did frankly give, and we did again travel on our journey to this supposed "Promised Land" (which better floweth with milk and honey, or I'm so returning-eth to Jerusalem ☺).

WHAT'S **REALLY** HAPPENING HERE

Laman and Lemuel are torn between two worlds:

Following their father to this **Promised Land**
-vs-
Enjoying their **Jerusalem lifestyle**

Doing what they know they **should be doing**
-vs-
Doing what they **really want** in their hearts

Their **righteous upbringing**
-vs-
Their **natural man tendencies**

Returning to Jerusalem and being reminded of their old lifestyle, L&L decide they want it back. Nephi sees where their hearts are and tells them, "And now, if ye have choice, go up to the land [Jerusalem], and remember the words which I speak unto you." In essence saying to them, *"Hey, go ahead and go back if you want. You're big boys, you can choose. But, remember, I told you so!"* So, here's the million-dollar question:

Why didn't L&L just go back home and bag this whole "Promised Land" field trip???

Because they are torn. They have too much of their **good** upbringing in them to fully rebel and return to Jerusalem. But they also have too much of their **bad** (natural man) tendencies to fully commit themselves to this Promised Land journey. In short, they are too scared to completely devote themselves to either the good **OR** the bad. They are stuck in the middle . . . riding the fence.

So often we play the game called *"Doing the Church Thing Mostly But We're Not Going to Entirely Devote Ourselves to God."* (Yeah, it has a long title. But quite descriptive, wouldn't you say?)

We try to play both sides. We'll be good and follow God . . . *unless* there's something else we really want, just for a moment, or just for a night, and then we'll make an exception. We'll be true to the faith . . . *unless* things get really hard, then we'll murmur or give into temptation. Dude . . . that is so Lemuel!

Don't ride the fence, my friend! Pick a side! Choose ye this day whom you will serve. And then devote *all* of you to that side.

"**KNEW NOT** THE DEALINGS OF THAT GOD WHO HAD CREATED THEM"

Nephi is amazed at his brothers' fence-riding ability. He asks them *three* times *"How is it that ye have forgotten?"* Forgotten that . . . 1) you saw an angel; 2) we *did* get the plates from Laban after all; and 3) the Lord can do *all* things if we are faithful to him (1 Nephi 7:10–12).

Well, Nephi, perhaps L&L have forgotten because they don't *try* to remember "the dealings of that God who had created them" and how He has helped them. Remembering takes effort. Without this effort, our minds seem pre-programmed to forget spiritual things, to stop acknowledging God's blessings, and to start slacking on our convictions.

THAT WAS **THEN** THIS IS **NOW**

In your journey through life, how can you "remember" and keep "the vision" fresh in your heart?

Well, once you've caught the vision, you'll need constant reminders of that vision or it <u>will</u> start to fade away. I mentioned this in the first chapter.

For example: <u>Before</u> the brothers were commanded to go back and get Ishmael's family, how was each of them using their time?

Nephi? He was enjoying some serious scripture bonding time with Dad (see 1 Nephi 5 & 6). They were totally into it: "searching" their newly obtained set of scriptures, probably marking them up with a highlighter engraving pen, finding "that they were desirable" and "of great worth." And then Nephi gets into his journal. He writes about how "the fulness of mine intent is to persuade men to come [to God]" and how "the things which are pleasing unto the world I do not write, but the things which are pleasing unto God and unto those who are not of this world."

What about Laman & Lemuel? How were they using their time? Who knows . . . maybe playing Hebrew Fortnite?

In other words: **Nephi CHOOSES to use his "free time" doing something that builds himself up spiritually.**

Is that so weird? It's such a simple concept, and yet for teenagers, it can be so foreign to you.

Nephi got in the habit of loving the things of the Spirit when he was young. Using his free time to feed his spirit comes naturally to him. He continually reminds himself that he is NOT of this world. He belongs to God. By so doing, he is solidifying the vision in his heart. No gospel fence riding here!

When you have free time, what do you **choose** to do? Or when you don't have "free time" because life is so busy, what do you **make** time to do? It's true that in our day you have a lot more distractions available to you. But do you have to give into them? Isn't it really about making a choice? How you spend your free time is entirely up to you.

Now, of course, we can still have fun. Our lives need to have balance. But next time you have free time and feel like spending hours doing something basically meaningless, remember this phrase:

"You can't kill time without injuring eternity."

When I was about seventeen, I had a friend named Eldon who taught me this concept just by the way he was.

We were in the same group at an Especially For Youth conference. The first night there, during a counselor devotional, the counselor asked all of us how we felt about our testimonies. While most of us hemmed and hawed, giving mediocre responses, Eldon genuinely expressed how much he loved the gospel and how it meant everything to him. He had been feeding his spirit long before EFY.

That week, Eldon used to initiate things like group scripture study amongst our group of guys. He wasn't embarrassed. The counselor didn't "put him up to it." He just loved the scriptures and assumed everyone else did too. He loved feeding his spirit.

After the week ended, we kept in touch through this ancient means called mail. Yeah, you might have read about it in your history books. His letters were full of things like, "Hey, have you heard this church music tape? [Yeah, tapes—another ancient relic.] It's awesome!" or "I was just reading this cool scripture, check it out!" And he was cool about it. Nothing weird.

Eldon taught me that the Church isn't just a side thing that you do the bare minimum with . . . while you spend the bulk of your time and efforts focusing on the things that you think *"really matter"* (like sports or your social life). The gospel WAS his focus. Like Nephi, he used his free time to feed his spirit, and he was one of the happiest guys I knew.

HOW 'BOUT THAT **NEPHI**

I think one of the true signs of our character is how we treat our family members . . . especially during the teenage years. I mean, we love our families more than anybody, but aren't they the hardest to love sometimes? We've all been there. Disagreements, power struggles, mean words, hurt feelings—these things can creep into any family setting if we're not careful. But have you ever had your siblings tie you up and leave you to be eaten by wild beasts in the wilderness?? (I hope you answered no.)

The following phrase in this story is testament to Nephi's character:

"And it came to pass that I did frankly forgive them all that they had done." (1 Nephi 7:21)

Wow. You mean even though they tried to kill him, Nephi

forgives his older brothers the instant they humbly ask for it? He doesn't mull it over? He doesn't think, "Hmm, but do they REALLY mean it?" or "Okay, but I can't forgive EVERYTHING they've done?" You mean he loves his jerky brothers that much? Yup. Crazy, huh?

Nephi frankly forgives L&L *all* that they had done to him, and they move on. "Water under the bridge," as they say.

When disagreements arise in your family, how quick are *you* to forgive? Can you do it? Or do you enjoy simmering in your bitterness until you've cooked up a nice batch of grudge gruel?

Just remember Scripture Mastery Doctrine and Covenants 64:9–11: "I, the Lord, will forgive whom I will forgive, but of you it is required to forgive all men" (and yes, that includes siblings!).

NEPHI'S QUOTABLE QUOTE

But it came to pass that I prayed unto the Lord, saying: O Lord, according to my faith which is in thee, wilt thou deliver me from the hands of my brethren; yea, even give me strength that I may burst these bands with which I am bound.

And it came to pass that when I had said these words, behold, the bands were loosed from off my hands and feet. (1 Nephi 7:17–18)

"**Burst** these bands!" Now that would have looked really cool! Like He-Man or something! But, hey . . . **loosening** the bands still has the same effect—it's just not as dramatic.

What a great reminder that Heavenly Father doesn't always answer our prayers the way **we** think He should answer them . . . but he DOES answer them.

BY THE WAY

Did you ever stop to think what an impossible task the *second* trip back to Jerusalem would have been? To convince a father to abandon everything and take his whole family into the life-threatening wilderness for the rest of their lives, to journey to some mysterious Promised Land . . . and do so based solely on *your* word that it is God's will? (Remember, Ishmael didn't have a personal vision of Jerusalem's destruction like Lehi did.) Wow! How did sons of Lehi do it?!

In 1 Nephi 7:4–5, Nephi simply says, *"And it came to pass that we went up unto the house of Ishmael, insomuch that we did speak unto him the words of the Lord. And it came to pass that the Lord did soften the heart of Ishmael, and also his household, insomuch that they took their journey with us."*

First of all, who do you think did most of the talking? Yup, I think so too. But who does Nephi give credit to? "We." In humility, he acknowledges the groups' efforts and the Lord's power, not his own abilities.

Yet we know it was Nephi's ability to speak with the power of God that was the reason for their success. Had Nephi not been filling his life with the Spirit, they would have probably failed.

Do you want more power to persuade people? Power to persuade your peers for good? Then get the Spirit . . . like Nephi! The Holy Ghost enhances everything about you, so that people will want to be around you. They will listen to you. They will want to do what you do. They'll see that you are different . . . a *good* kind of different . . . and will want that for themselves.

SUMMING IT UP

Doctor's Report

Disease LEMUELITIS as shown by . . .

"Gospel Fence Riding"

Symptoms - Going back and forth from good to bad, not committing to either one

- Forgetting all the good things God has given you
- Anger at those who remind you of what you should be doing

Prescription Keep your vision . . . by using your free time to feed your spirit

Dr. Bowman

Signature

Chapter 4

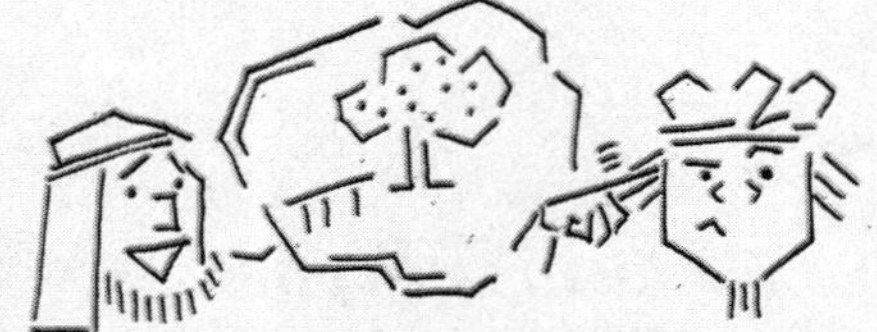

Dad Sure Has Some Strange Dreams

(Nephi's version—1 Nephi 8, 10, 15, 16:1–6)

And it came to pass that our Father did awake one morning, crying with a loud voice, saying: **Behold, I have dreamed a dream, yea, I have seen a vision!** And Laman and I spake unto each other, rolling our eyes, even with a great roll, saying: **Here we goeth again!**

And it came to pass that our Father spake of his dream, saying: **Behold, in my dream, I saw a large field, with numberless concords of people, pressing foreheads, that they might catch hold of the iron ram, that would lead them through the mitts of darkness, away from some great and delicious building, filled with people who were coughing at them, yea, and the iron ram did lead them safely to the tree of lights, that they might partake of the fruit that was really, really white and exceedingly yummy.**

(Okay, so I wasn't really listening, except for the part about food).

NEVERTHELESS, IN FATHER'S DREAM, LAMAN AND I DID NOT PARTAKE OF THE FRUIT. WHATEVER-ETH.

AND AS I, LEMUEL, WAS ABOUT TO TURN AWAY, YEA, TO SEEK OUT SOMETHING TO EAT, BEHOLD, MY FATHER DID LAY HOLD UPON MY SHOULDER, AND THE SHOULDER OF MY BROTHER LAMAN, AND DID LOOK US IN THE EYES, PLEADING WITH US TO LISTEN TO HIS WORDS AND HEARKEN UNTO THE LORD, FOR VERILY HE FEARED LEST WE BE CUT OFF FOREVER, YEA, HE DID GET ALL EMOTIONAL ON US, PREACHING AND NAGGING, INSOMUCH THAT I WONDERED, **How much longer is this going to taketh?!,** FOR I WAS EXCEEDINGLY HUNGRY.

NEVERTHELESS, MY HOPE WAS IN VAIN, FOR MY FATHER DID CONTINUE TO RAMBLE ON FOR THE SPACE OF MANY HOURS CONCERNING GENTILES, AND JEWS, AND OLIVE TREES, AND BRANCHES, AND PROMISED LANDS; YEA, INSOMUCH THAT MY EYES DID GLAZE OVER, AND GREAT WAS THE MIST OF BOREDOM WHICH DID DESCEND UPON ME.

AND IT CAME TO PASS THAT MY FATHER DID FINALLY CEASE SPEAKING UNTO US. AND THERE WAS MUCH REJOICING.

AND IT CAME TO PASS THAT SOME TIME LATER, KNOW-IT-ALL NEPHI DID TRY TO EXPLAIN THE MEANING OF MY FATHER'S WORDS UNTO US, SAYING: **Have ye inquired of the Lord of their meaning?** DUH! OF COURSE NAY, NEPHI! THAT TAKETH TOO MUCH WORK.

AND NEPHI CEASED NOT SPEAKING UNTO US UNTIL HE HAD TAKEN US ON A THOROUGH GUILT TRIP, TELLING US THAT WICKED PEOPLE DON'T GO TO HEAVEN AND OTHER SHOCKING NEWS OF THAT NATURE, YEA, INSOMUCH THAT I DID COMMENCE FEELING BAD AGAIN FOR THE THINGS I HAD DONE.

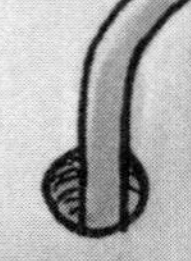

O, how great the strangeness of that feeling, yea, even the feeling of guilt! How weird it is to actually want to follow the Lord and be good, yea, how . . . how . . . uh . . . umm . . . what was I saying? Hmm, uh, oh well. I hungereth. When's dinner?

WHAT'S **REALLY** HAPPENING HERE

This is an interesting scenario in chronicles of Lehi Family Robinson.

The Lord gives **Lehi** this awesome vision of the tree of life (1 Nephi 8). You are probably familiar with this vision, but it's worth another read.

Nephi experiences his own incredible vision that expounds on the things his father saw (1 Nephi 11–14).

But what about **L&L**?? What do they experience? Surprisingly, more than you might think.

When Lehi tells his sons about his dream, L&L may not have the spiritual maturity of a Nephi (that is, to seek knowledge from the Spirit on their own), but they don't entirely blow it off either. As usual, they're stuck somewhere in-between . . . ridin' the fence. They debate with each other over what the dream means, go around in circles, and get nowhere.

Finally, instead of turning to the Lord for answers, L&L turn to Nephi to explain the dream to them. And the amazing thing is, by the time Nephi is finished, L&L are actually feeling the Spirit! I know, you can pick your jaw up off the ground now. 😊 As a matter of fact, Nephi says **twice** that his brothers "did humble themselves before the Lord" and then adds "insomuch that I had joy and great hopes of them, that they would walk in the paths of righteousness" (1 Nephi 16:5).

In other words, this is no small deal! Nephi truly believes this to be the turning point for his hard-hearted brothers.

So, what happened? Why didn't this "turning point" stick? Perhaps, because L&L . . .

"**KNEW NOT** THE DEALINGS OF THAT GOD WHO HAD CREATED THEM"

Nephi hopes that L&L's "**humbling themselves before the Lord**" will **LEAD TO** their "**walking in the paths of righteousness.**" Sometimes we think those two ideas are the same thing . . . but they're not.

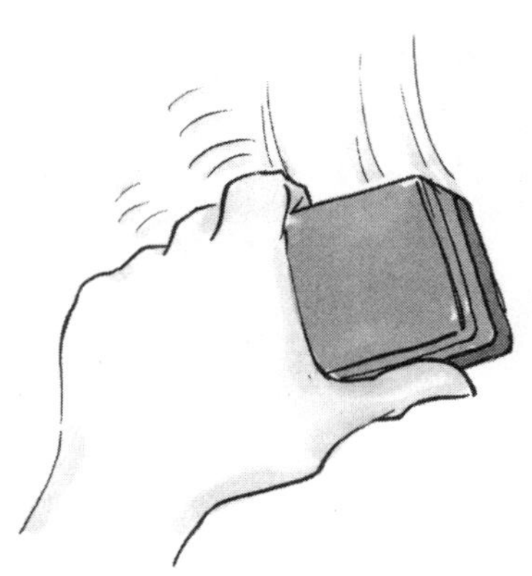

Think of it this way. Humbling yourself is like **ERASING** all the pride and junk off the slate of your heart. It's coming to the realization that you need God. It's a start. It needs to happen. Focused settings where the Spirit is present (such as youth conferences, girls' camps, EFYs, and so on) are common places for this humbling to occur. Once your slate is wiped clean, you are ready for Heavenly Father to start working his great design in your life.

BUT . . . it is your consistent *righteous living* that allows Heavenly Father *access* to your slate . . . where He can start **ADDING** to you! That's when His skilled strokes and perfect vision can make a masterpiece of your life. In other words, its what you do **after** an EFY experience that really matters!

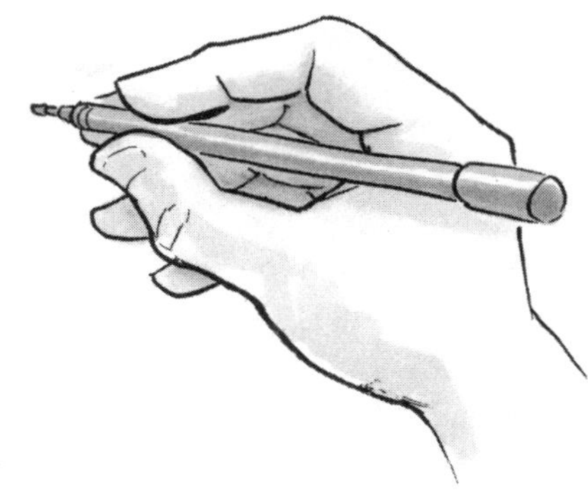

It appears that L&L erased the pride & junk off the slates of their hearts, but never took it to the next step (that is, walking in righteousness). They kept their slates blank, until by and by, they just went back to their prideful ways.

Hey! There's a great lesson to be learned here: The next time *you* have one of those humbling "I better get my act together" experiences, what should you do? Hmm . . . oh, I dunno . . . maybe . . . **DO IT!**

DUDE! DON'T BE A LEMUEL

Imagine this conversation between two classmates:

Huh? Come again? Did that last line even make any sense to you? I hope not.

But that is exactly what L&L tell Nephi when they mention how they don't understand Lehi's words. Nephi asks them, "Have ye inquired of the Lord?" Lemon and Lamo respond with, "We have not; for the Lord maketh no such thing known unto us" (1 Nephi 15:7–9).

Dude, don't be a Lemuel! Don't say stupid things that don't make sense! Don't expect the Lord to just give you something on a silver platter . . . without any effort on your part. Don't expect your seminary or Sunday school teachers to just give you a spiritual experience . . . without your participation and focus. Don't expect to get your own testimony . . . without working consistently for it yourself.

I love how Nephi just lets 'em have it (in vs. 10–11) after that classic Lemuel-ism. "How is it that ye are such knuckleheads?!" he says, in more or less words. ☺

NEPHI'S QUOTABLE QUOTE

For he that diligently seeketh shall find; and the mysteries of God shall be unfolded unto him, by the power of the Holy Ghost. (1 Nephi 10:19)

This is Nephi's mantra. He believes it, he lives it, he gets it.

> Revelation is communication from Heavenly Father to His children on earth. As we ask in faith, we can receive revelation upon revelation and knowledge upon knowledge and come to know the mysteries and peaceable things that bring joy and eternal life.
>
> (Elder David A. Bednar, "Pray Always," *Ensign*, Nov. 2008)

HOW 'BOUT THAT **NEPHI**

Let's say it again: How . . . About . . . That . . . Nephi! In 1 Nephi 11–14, Nephi puts into action his belief that when you diligently seek, the mysteries of God *will* be shown to you. And were they ever!

After listening to his father's dream, Nephi wants to understand its meaning for himself. He ponders it. He pleads for understanding. He is "caught away in the Spirit of the Lord . . . into an exceedingly high mountain." And that is where an angel shows Nephi the deeper meaning of Lehi's dream . . . <u>and</u> a whole lot more. It's like Nephi ordered a Tree of Life combo . . . and then the Lord supersized it! 😊

There's not enough room in this book to go into all the details of Nephi's vision. You get to feast on them on your own (1 Nephi 11–14)! Lucky you!

But I do want to hit one point: What is the *greatest* thing Nephi got out of his visionary experience?

He came to know Christ.

In 1 Nephi 11, the very first thing Nephi's angelic guide focuses on is the tree.

That most beautiful of all trees, with pure white fruit that is more delicious than anything Nephi's ever tasted. It represents the love of God. And how did God show that He so loved the world? By giving His only begotten Son (John 3:16). So, the love of God is Jesus Christ. The tree is Christ.

Then, just to help Nephi gain a deeper understanding of this love, the angel gives Nephi a panoramic vision of Jesus's life: His birth. His baptism. His teachings. His ministerings. His healings. His trial. His crucifixion. Nephi sees it all (1 Nephi. 11:12–33). Can you imagine how Nephi must be feeling? He just saw his Savior suffer and die . . . for HIM. He watched it happen. Nephi describes his feeling in verse 22, "Yea, [*I feel*] the love of God, which sheddeth itself abroad in [my heart], wherefore it is the most desirable above all things."

Can't you just see Nephi? He's completely overcome with love and joy. I picture the angel smiling, patting Nephi's shoulder, and saying, "Yea, and the most joyous to the soul" (v. 23), as if to say "I know, Nephi . . . Isn't it the greatest feeling?" I love this part!

THAT WAS **THEN** THIS IS **NOW**

Have you felt the love of Christ?

When all is said and done, I think Nephi's whole purpose in writing to us is to help us feel that love . . . like he himself feels. He even said so. "We talk of Christ, we rejoice in Christ, we preach of Christ, we prophesy of Christ, and we write according to our prophecies, *that our children* [or plug in your own name] *may know to what source they may look for a remission of their sins*" (2 Nephi 25:26).

Nephi knows that feeling the Love of Christ is the most liberating, most refreshing, most precious, most inspiring, most indescribably **GOOD** feeling in the world! That's just it—it's impossible to describe! You have to experience it for yourself.

And you **can** experience it for yourself! Just listen to the rest of Nephi's Quotable Quote:

"For he that diligently seeketh shall find; and the mysteries of God shall be unfolded unto him, by the power of the Holy Ghost, ***as well in these times as in times of old, and as well in times of old as in times to come; wherefore, the course of the Lord is one eternal round.***" (1 Nephi 10:19)

It doesn't matter who you are, where you live, or when you lived . . . Heavenly Father's mysteries are available to anyone who diligently seeks them. Anytime. Anywhere. He is eager to bless us with spiritual enlightenment as soon as we qualify to receive it. On occasion, this enlightenment comes through powerful experiences (like Nephi had). But more often than not, it comes little by little, in small quiet impressions from the spirit.

And, as Nephi discovered, the greatest of all the mysteries of God is His love, shown through the Atonement of His Son. Your journey through life is totally meaningless without feeling His love. Seek it for yourself.

SUMMING IT UP

Doctor's Report

Disease LEMUELITIS as shown by . . .
"Making no effort to seek out spiritual knowledge for yourself"

Symptoms
- Spiritual laziness
- Expecting others to give you a testimony or a spiritual experience
- Not following up with action when you do feel spiritual promptings

Prescription Make that EXTRA effort in your search for spiritual knowledge . . . (especially through scripture study and personal prayer/pondering time)

Dr. Bowman

Signature

YOUR DOSAGE OF SCRIPTURE POWER

MORONI 10:4–5

REFILL AS OFTEN AS NEEDED

HALFTIME!

Brought to you by . . .

One evening, an apartment of female BYU students receives this note on their front doorstep . . .

Intrigued, the young ladies decide to follow the instructions. They walk to the designated tree and wait. "Okay, now what," they think.

Suddenly, a heavenly being, dressed in a glowing white robe, appears before them. In a majestic voice, he calls the girls by name and declares that he was sent to them with a very important message. "There is a record," he proclaims, "written upon sacred plates, buried in this very sand, right underneath the volleyball net. Go forth and find it." And with that, the messenger vanishes out of sight!

Well, he actually just scurries away behind some bushes. And his glowing white robe looks more like a bedsheet with someone shining a flashlight on it. (Okay, it is a bedsheet with someone shining a flashlight on it). And his voice isn't very majestic, and his being isn't very heavenly. In fact, he looks a lot like my roommate, Matt!

The group of girls chuckles at the "angel" and begins searching for the buried record. In a minute or so, they find it. They are plates, all right. Round, thin . . . *paper* plates. There's an inscription on them, written in ancient Sharpie marker:

That Saturday night, my roommates and I (the sons of Lehi) show up at the girls' apartment. We're decked out in robes and headbands—the works. The very first thing we do when they open the door is get down on one knee, hold out candy Ring Pops, and propose . . . thus, making these lovely daughters of Ishmael our wives. After all, it wouldn't be appropriate to travel to the Promised Land together *unmarried!*

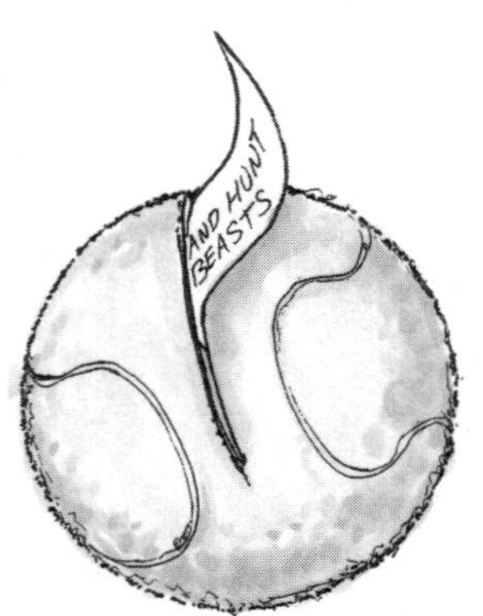

We even had our own **Liahona** to guide us on our journey *(Translation: We cut a slit in an old tennis ball and stuffed little slips of paper inside, each slip telling us what to do next on our journey).*

Here's a few of the things the "Liahona" instructed us to do that night:

—Witness the wickedness and greed of Jerusalem. *(Translation: We went to a public place, taped clear fishing line to a dollar bill, and placed it on the ground, while we sat inconspicuously at a side table. When passersby reached down to pick up the dollar, we gently tugged the line, keeping the dollar just out of reach of their greedy paws. Most of them would chuckle and just walk away, except for the last guy. I guess he was on to us because when he approached the dollar, he suddenly lunged forward, stepped on the bill before we could pull it away, whipped out a pocketknife, cut the string, took the dollar, and walked away. Okay, buddy, if you want it that much, it's yours.)*

—Go hunt for food *(Translation: A game of darts, with drawings of wild beasts placed over the dartboard)*

—Walk blindly across the wilderness *(Translation: A three-legged couples race across the entire BYU campus . . . with both of you blindfolded! Now, that took some skill and cooperation)*

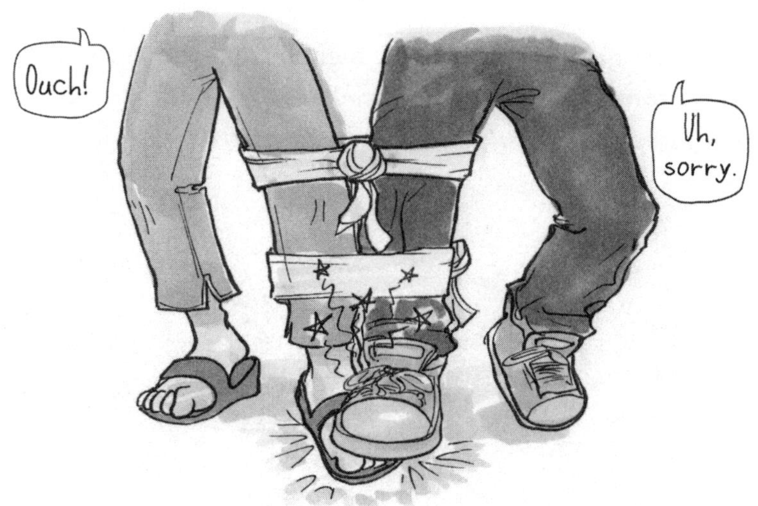

—**Build ships and sail across the ocean** *(Translation: Couples constructed tiny rafts out of sticks and twine and raced them down a stream. And to make it more interesting, each raft had to carry two large marshmallows that the couple had to eat at the end of the race . . . ya know, extra incentive to build a raft that wouldn't tip over. And, of course, our raft tipped over. Mmmm . . . soggy, water-logged marshmallow)*

—And finally, we finished the night by **receiving refreshment in the Promised Land** *(Translation: Denny's . . . the promised land of late night dining. Milk and honey was ordered by all).*

See, my friend, even dating can be more fun when you "liken the scriptures unto ourselves." ☺

All right, let's get back to the story . . .

Chapter 5

Broken Bows & Hunger Woes

(Nephi's version—1 Nephi 16:6–39)

And it came to pass that I did take the hottest of the daughters of Ishmael to wife. Aaaahh yeeaaahh!

And it came to pass that we did pack up our tents and did take our journey into the wilderness, leaving **MY** valley, yea, the Valley of **LEMUEL**, yea, the **Greatest valley IN THE WORLD,** yea, even greater than the river of Laman which floweth through it!! HA!

FOR BEHOLD I AM LEMUEL AND I AM A MORON!!

And it came to pass that Laman wrote that last part when I wasn't looking, yea, it grieveth me that I cannot eraseth words on these plates.

And it came to pass that before we took our journey into the wilderness, lo and behold, our father did find a brass ball outside his tent. And it had spindles, and wherever they pointed we did journey in that direction, and thus ye see, we have ALL gone a little loony by now.

Now it came to pass that after traveling for the space of many days, and while hunting for food, behold, clutzy Nephi did break his steel bow, yea, his large in stature arms did snap that bow right in two!

Wherefore, Nephi doth continue to be the cause of all our problems, yea, he hath caused us to be exceedingly hungry, for we have no food, and he hath caused us to be exceedingly grumpy, for all things are his fault, and he hath also caused mine and Laman's bows to lose their springs because he doth not stop us from doing stupid things with our bows.

(What if they could **Facebook** back then?)

News Feed

Top News • Most Recent 6

Share: Status Photo Link Video Question

What's on your mind?

Lemuel

This is so lame! Now Nephi just broke his bow and we have like NO FOOD!! Can you believe it?? I even caught his bow breaking on my phone. Yea, epic fail. Can't wait till we can go back home to Jerusalem and end this "Family bonding time" trip.

Watch youtube clip
www.youtube.com

 23 hours ago · Like · Comment

 47 people like this.

 View all 7 comments

Wicked and proud of it Ha ha! You guys are nuts out there! Way to go Nephi!
21 hours ago · Like

Livin' the Good life Well, nowz your chance to diet and lose those chubby cheeks of yours, Lemuel. Ha Ha! Dude, you missed a killer party last night. We used your Dad's house.
20 hours ago · Like

Exceedingly Fair Cheerleader Ooohh! Oh No! Just make sure Laman's okay . . . I miss him so much! Give him hugs for me.
17 hours ago · Like

Lemuel

Check out this ridiculous bow Nephi made out of some stick. He thinks he can actually go hunting with this thing. Ha ha.

Mobile Uploads

 2 hours ago · Like · Comment

 31 people like this.

 View all 4 comments

Born to be Wild HA HA HA HA HA HA HA HA HA HA HA HA!!!!
49 minutes ago · Like

Wicked and proud of it Wow! You gotta be kidding. Nephi couldn't even earn the archery merit badge at Hebrew scout camp a few summers ago. Good luck! You're all toast! :)
18 minutess ago · Like

And while we were thus indulging in our pity pot, behold, Nephi did go forth and make a new bow and arrow out wood, and did ask father where he should go to find food.

And Laman and I did laugh his new bow to scorn, for behold, IT WAS A PIECE OF JUNK, yea, Nephi could not hit the broad side of a synagogue with that thing, let alone get us dinner.

And it came to pass that Nephi did somehow COMPLETELY, TOTALLY, AMAZINGLY LUCK OUT _AGAIN_, and he did slay wild beasts with his new bow, insomuch that he did obtain food for everyone, And after we did pick our jaws up from off the ground, we did use them to feast upon the wild beasts, and great was the grub mowing thereof!

But behold, our joy lasted for only a short season, because of the death of Ishmael shortly thereafter, and great was our bummed-ness again.

And wo be unto us, for behold, WE HAVE SUFFERED MUCH, EVEN HUNGER, AND THIRST, AND FATIGUE, AND KINKS IN OUR NECKS SO THAT THEY ARE STIFF, and Nephi's positive attitude, and no cell phone reception, and every manner of affliction. And Laman spake unto me and the others saying: **Let us slay our father and Nephi, who hath taken it upon himself to be our ruler.**

Now, he says that the Lord and angels have talked with him. But behold, we know that this is exceedingly bogus, for all Nephi wants to do is boss us around, and be our ruler, yea, he thinketh he is so cool, and doth force us to be out here with him, and is tricking us because I am stupid, or I

mean he thinketh I am stupid, insomuch that . . . (BLAH, BLAH, BLAH-ETH)

AND IT CAME TO PASS THAT THE VOICE OF THE LORD SPAKE UNTO US AND DID LET US HAVE IT, AND WE DID SHUT UP FOR A SEASON.

WHAT'S **REALLY** HAPPENING HERE

Ahh yes, the story of the broken bow. A classic case of . . . do you **ACT** or do you *REACT*?

What do I mean by that? Well, imagine a marionette.

A skilled puppeteer can tug and pull those strings until you forget that it's even a puppet! It looks so alive! But is it alive? Does a marionette, in and of itself, have any life whatsoever? No. Its only actions are REACTIONS. REACTIONS to somebody else "pulling its strings." The only puppet I've heard of who truly knew how to ACT, not just REACT, was named Pinocchio. (All right, everybody sing with me! "I got no strings to hold me down" ♫☺).

Breaking a bow, getting the brass plates, leaving Jerusalem—these are just situations (albeit challenging ones) where each member of Lehi's family has a choice to make: Do I ACT . . . or do I REACT? Am I in control of my responses? Or do I just go with my initial gut reaction without thinking?

Lemuel, dude, you are the KING of REACTING! You let Laman pull your strings by simply doing whatever he wants! And Laman, you are just as bad. Something hard comes along, and all you do is REACT with murmuring, anger, violence, jealousy, name-calling, and overall grumpiness. ☹ BOTH of you let yourselves be yanked around by whatever stimulus comes your way:

"Nephi, my YOUNGER brother, is telling ME what I should do?!?! . . . Oohh, that makes me so mad! (Even if he is right)."

"You still wanna go back and try to get those plates from Laban?!?! . . . No way, that's impossible! Forget it! (Even if we did just see an angel)."

"You just broke your bow, Nephi?!?! . . . That's it! We're dead! Game over! Aaarrgghh!"

Basically, L&L did not understand how agency works.

Lame guys. Lame.

"KNEW NOT THE DEALINGS OF THAT GOD WHO HAD CREATED THEM"

You are Heavenly Father's spirit child. As such, he has given you agency. It is the power to act, to do, to think whatever you choose . . . regardless of what other people are doing, regardless of the circumstance you are in, regardless of how strong a temptation is, regardless of your past mistakes. YOU CHOOSE!

"Yeah, but what if a situation is SO BAD that you just **have to** REACT negatively to it?" you might ask. "Like, what if you were put in a Nazi concentration camp in World War II, had all your freedoms taken away, were starved, beaten, and had all your loved ones taken from you and killed . . . all simply because you were a Jew. How could *anyone* not REACT with bitterness and hatred to *that* kind of unfair treatment?"

Well, a man named Viktor Frankl did just that. He endured everything you just mentioned and did not turn to anger and bitterness. In fact, listen to some of the things he said later in life about agency:

> Between stimulus and response there is a space. In that space is our power to choose our response. In our response lies our growth and our freedom.
>
> Everything can be taken from a man or a woman but one thing: the last of human freedoms to choose one's attitude in any given set of circumstances, to choose one's own way.

Hmm. So, what were you saying about how it's too hard to not REACT sometimes? ☺

THAT WAS **THEN** THIS IS **NOW**

My young friends, in your journey through life, if you can catch on to this concept of ACTing and not REACTing *as a teenager* . . . you will be so much further ahead of 99 percent of your peers. It will forever change how you look at life—spiritually, emotionally, socially, intellectually, and physically. You will become the type of person who makes things happen. You will lead. It is a rare, inspiring thing to see someone who ACTS and doesn't REACT . . . especially at your age.

Three categories in which Satan tempts us to REACT instead of ACT that we need to watch out for are. . .

1) **OTHER PEOPLE:**

"Well, she didn't apologize, so I'm just gonna ignore her."

"He makes me so mad! I'm not even gonna talk to him."

"I'm not gonna say 'hi' to her. I don't even know her! She might think I'm weird."

"Well, everyone's doing it . . . so I better just go along."

"He's so good at this. I'll never be as good as him. Why do I even bother?"

Do these phrases sound normal to you? Probably. But they are all REACTIONS. They are letting someone else control what we do or how we feel about ourselves. We subconsciously say to ourselves "Well, if they're doing 'X' . . . then I'm gonna do 'Y.' " Most of us don't even realize when we are letting someone else pull our strings. REACTING comes automatically.

We throw out phrases like, "I just can't help it" or "That makes me so mad," as if there is some other power in control of our actions. My friend, nothing has the power to "make" you mad . . . or make you anything, for that matter. You CHOOSE these responses. You CHOOSE your emotions. It sounds crazy, but it's true.

> We have far more control over our happiness than we sometimes think we do. How we see life's glass—half-full or half-empty—is primarily a choice.
>
> (Elder Lynn G. Robbins, "True Beauty," *New Era*, Nov. 2008)

2) **CIRCUMSTANCES:**

Circumstances are things like where you are born, situations you're in, things that happen to you, your upbringing, your raw talents and abilities (or lack of raw talent). People love to REACT by blaming their circumstances for their unhappiness and their failures. Dude, that is so Lemuel.

How 'bout when something "bad" happens to you? How do you respond to trials and challenges? Do you just complain and make excuses for giving up (REACT)? OR do you rise *above* the bad stuff and let those things make you stronger (ACT)?

Like Honest Abe.

Do you know how many times Abraham Lincoln failed before he became president? A lot! Look it up. However, he didn't let his circumstances dictate his destiny. Every time he failed, he got back up and tried again. And he became one of our nation's greatest presidents.

You determine your destiny.

3) **PAST EXPERIENCE:**

Sometimes it isn't other people or circumstances that we REACT to; it's our past experience.

For example: Do you let the mistakes of your past hold you back from becoming the person God knows you can be? Have you decided that "Hey, I'm just not good at 'X'!" or "I'll never be able to quit my bad habit of 'Y'"? Have you responded to Satan's temptation to REACT with hopelessness and despair when you sin?

Please, friend . . . **do not let your past hold your future hostage!** Did you get that? I'm gonna say that again . . . **do not let your past hold your future hostage!**

Your Savior, Jesus Christ, paid the ultimate price so that through repentance, any unwanted baggage of your past can be eliminated. Gone! Permanently! Whoosh! You have no excuses. Your future is bright and it is unwritten . . . regardless of your past. That's the "good news" of the gospel.

THE BOOK OF **BOWMAN**

I remember one time as a teenager when I tried out this "ACT, don't REACT" concept. My mom and I were having an argument about something. I don't remember what about, probably something I did, but that's not important. We were both REACTing to anger at this point. Voice levels were rising. Tempers were flaring. And the natural response would be to keep going at it until someone stormed out of the room in a huff, slammed a door, and . . . well, you probably know how it works. 😊

I'm not sure why, but for some reason this time, as I was looking at my mom's angry expression, a thought pop into my head, "Man, my mom sure does love me." So, instead of continuing the pride battle, I just said flat out, "Mom, I love you."

Well, after the paramedics revived her . . . j/k ☺. After I said that, she was speechless for a moment. And then she said, "I love you too." It was like we both suddenly realized that what we were arguing about wasn't important and that our relationship was. It was amazing the power that ACTing (instead of REACTing) had on the situation.

HOW 'BOUT THAT **NEPHI**

Do you know what really impresses me about Nephi here?

It's not just his ability to ACT and find a solution to the problem while his brothers are whining. Of course L&L are gonna murmur, that's expected. It's his ability to ACT when the *entire family group* (including father Lehi) starts murmuring against the Lord (see 1 Nephi 16:20).

Put yourself in Nephi's sandals:

Here's your Father . . . the head of the family, a prophet, a spiritual giant, the one who you have trusted faithfully ever since he first announced this family journey. And in a moment of weakness, *he too* does the natural response and starts to REACT by murmuring against the Lord. How easy would it be to just go along and say, "Well, if *Dad* is murmuring, than I guess it's okay if we all start murmuring a little. I mean, don't we have a right to complain just a tad? This *IS* hard, after all!"

But did Nephi go along with everyone's negative REACTions? Nope, not even "a little." Nephi isn't just piggy-backing off of his parent's testimony. His trust in the Lord is not based on other people. He is his own man. His "vision" is intact. And Nephi knows how to ACT . . . regardless of the situation or how others are acting.

NEPHI'S QUOTABLE QUOTE

And it came to pass that I, Nephi, did make out of wood a bow, and out of a straight stick, and arrow; . . . And I said unto my father: Whither shall I go to obtain food? (1 Nephi 16:23)

And then, even after Lehi's murmuring, Nephi still respects his father's role as prophet and patriarch of the family by turning to him for hunting directions. He didn't just say, "Well, Dad's complaining now also, so I guess I'm on my own with this one."

Perhaps Nephi realized that this time, the son could actually build up his own father. Perhaps he realized that Lehi, in a time of weakness, would need this reassurance and strengthening from his boy. It sure inspired Lehi and helped him get out of the funk he was in.

Your parents aren't perfect, you guys. Don't expect them to be. There may be times when they don't lead out perfectly in everything. When they go through a moment of weakness, then YOU humbly step up to the plate and be *their* example for a change. They will love you for it!

BY THE WAY

Before we finish this chapter, please remember that ACTing/ REACTing are states of mind that all people go in and out of. Nobody ACTS perfectly all the time, without ever REACTing. I certainly don't. It's not easy to do. Even Nephi admits to REACTing at times (check out 2 Nephi 4:26–29). So, don't get discouraged. My purpose in bringing all this up is awareness. So that the next time a situation arises where REACTing with an automatic negative response would be so easy, you might think again and choose to ACT instead.

But here's a helpful hint: When the spirit of Christ is in your heart, ACTing becomes so much easier to do . . . almost second nature.

SUMMING IT UP

Doctor's Report

Disease LEMUELITIS as shown by . . .
"REACTing, instead of ACTing"

Symptoms - Tendency to go with your natural, negative response in any given situation
- Anger, whining, complaining, jealousy, depression, fear, and every other "yucky" emotion
- Never taking the initiative to make something happen

Prescription ACT . . . by getting the spirit of Christ in your heart

Dr. Bowman

Signature

Chapter 6

You Wanna Build a WHAT?!

(Nephi's version—1 Nephi 17)

And it came to pass that 8 years came to pass.

And now I, Lemuel, have been short in writing for these past 8 years because my children have continually sat upon these plates, yea, even using these plates as a booster seat to partake of raw meat at the dinner table, insomuch that my wife (yea, I did marry the hottest of the daughters of Ishmael . . . did I mention that already?) and kids have become tougher than nails, and do bear their burdens without complaining.

NEVERTHELESS I AM STILL A WUSS AND HAVE BEEN FOREVER AND EVER AND WILL BE.

And my eldest brother, **LAME**-n, hath **AGAIN** engraven upon these plates when I wasn't looking. But behold, I did wrestle the engraving tool out of his hand, and did teach him a lesson grievous to be born, insomuch that he will durst not write upon these plates ever again!

ANYWAY . . . It came to pass that after 8 years, we did finally come to the seashore, and we did pitch our tents, and do now feast on much fruit, and wild honey, and coconut drinks with the little umbrellas in them, wherefore I do tarry here in my hammock, "chillin'" with an exceeding great chill, yea, thinking unto myself, **Perhaps this here "Promised Land" isn't so bad after all.**

And it came to pass that after I, Lemuel, had been beach-bummin' it for the space of many days, I did one day hearken unto a loud clanging sound in the distance. And as I did go forth with Laman to seek out the source of the sound thereof, behold, we did find Nephi, making tools out of ore.

And he did explain unto us that he was building a ship as the Lord had commanded him, that we all might sail together to the Promised Land, and he did exhort us to labor with him.

And we did exhort Nephi, with all the feelings of his tender brothers, to go jump in an Irreantum.

For behold, we have had <u>enough</u> of Nephi already; yea, my soul is rent with anguish because of him, and WO, WO, WO (yes, that's a triple "wo") be unto us for hearkening unto the multitude of his harebrained ideas thus far, for had we just stayed in Jerusalem, we could have been happy, howbeit all we have out here is sufferings and afflictions and chapped lips. So, helpeth you build a ship?! Ha! I think "Nay"! Uh-uh. No help from us. No way, Jose. No chance, Sundance. Nice try, Nephi! I mean it! Anybody wanna a peanut? Amen, and amen. Thus saith the Lemuel.

Nevertheless, Nephi could not forbear from tormenting us with yet another one of his tedious sermons, yea, even more tedious than all the sermons we had ever before heard coming forth from his mouth.

And now, as Laman and I went forth to assist our younger brother in fulfilling our previous exhortation, Nephi did stretch forth his hand and did cry with a loud voice, **Touch me not! For I am filled with the power of God! And if ye do touch me, it ain't gonna be pretty!**

And it came to pass that . . . And thus, we . . . Wherefore, I . . . Insomuch that . . . behold, he . . . uh . . . umm . . . Look, how do you respond to *THAT?!*

And thus we did steer clear of Nephi for a season, for behold, he was glowing n' stuff.

And after the space of many days, Nephi came unto us, and did stretch forth his hand to apologize to us, yea, his hand of mercy did extend toward me and it did . . . KKKZZZAAAAAAAPP!!!

YEEEEOOOOOWWWW!!

(What if this story were told anime style?)

AND IT CAME TO PASS THAT SUDDENLY BUILDING A SHIP DOESN'T SOUND SO BAD AFTER ALL.

WHAT'S **REALLY** HAPPENING HERE

Ahhh, the beach at last!

After eight long years of hardship in the wilderness, the group finally arrives at the ocean. And it's beautiful. There's fruit growing everywhere! There's wild honey. There's warm water. "This is where we can finally set up camp and relax," they think.

However, the Lord has something else in mind. Yes, He allows the group a little R&R (rest & relaxation), but the beach is NOT their new home. The Promised Land is. While Heavenly Father is preparing Nephi to build a ship to get them there, He is also preparing to build this family up to a whole new level of working together and trusting in Him. God is ready to deepen their discipleship . . . but are they ready?

DUDE! DON'T BE A LEMUEL

Well, as can be expected, guess who's not ready??

Yes, L&L have gotten used to their R&R at their B&B (Bed & Breakfast) by the seashore. They're content just to chill. So when Nephi approaches them about building a ship and sailing across unknown waters to God-only-knows-where (literally) . . . naturally, Laman & Lemuel are gonna throw a fit.

Check out the chain of arguments and rationalizations they use to justify themselves in not helping Nephi (1 Nephi 17:19–22):

> They play the **Belittle Spiritual Things** card: *"All these visions and promptings you & Dad have been claiming all along, they are totally just foolish imaginations!"* (v. 20)

They play the **Throw a Pity Party** card: *"Wo is us! We've gone through so much already. You can't possibly expect us to do this too!"* (vs. 20–21)

They play the **Call Evil Good** card: *"The people in Jerusalem weren't that bad! As a matter of fact, they were pretty righteous if you ask me! They totally kept the letter of the law of Moses."* (v. 22)

And the **Call Good Evil** card: *"You and Dad are the self-righteous ones! You are totally judging them. Sheesh!"* (v. 22)

L&L are trying so hard to convince themselves that it's okay if they don't obey the Lord. Dude, don't rationalize away doing something that you know is right simply because it's not convenient. That is so Lemuel!

But perhaps their murmuring runs a little deeper. Maybe what really paralyzes them is fear . . .

- **Fear of their inadequacy** (We have no clue how to build a ship! Can we succeed in actually building something that will be seaworthy for the entire journey?)
- **Fear of the unknown** (Does this Promised Land place even exist?).
- **Fear of change** (Beach, sand, sun, surf's up . . . Hey, why leave?)

And **fear** comes from **lack of trust** in Heavenly Father.

"KNEW NOT THE DEALINGS OF THAT GOD WHO HAD CREATED THEM"

Have you ever heard the expression "growing pains"? This quote from C.S. Lewis does a good job of explaining the kind of growing pains Heavenly Father has designed for you:

> Imagine yourself as a living house. God comes in to rebuild that house. At first, perhaps, you can understand what He is doing. He is getting the drains right and stopping the leaks in the roof and so on; you knew that those jobs needed doing and so you are not surprised. But presently He starts knocking the house about in a way that hurts abominably and does not seem to make any sense. What on earth is He up to? The explanation is that He is building quite a different house from the one you thought of—throwing out a new wing here, putting on an extra floor there, running up towers, making courtyards. You thought you were being made into a decent little cottage: but He is building a palace. He intends to come and live in it Himself.
>
> — C.S. Lewis, *Mere Christianity*

Your Father in Heaven is in the business of building . . . building up His children to be the very finest people they can be. He has the master architectural plans for your life, and the end product is a lot greater than a mere cottage. But before you can become that grand palace, you will experience a lot of growing pains along the way.

What Laman and Lemuel did not understand was this: That by trusting God and working together willingly to build this ship, they would actually be building themselves.

HOW 'BOUT THAT **NEPHI**

Let's not overlook what a TITANIC task it was to build this ship. (No pun intended. ☺) We're not just talkin' medium-sized boat . . . we're talkin' SHIP! BIG ship! One that . . .

— Is large enough to carry a few dozen people

—Has enough storage room for provisions to last them an entire YEAR at sea

—Will actually *stay afloat* for that entire year at sea

And to top it all off . . . Nephi has zero shipbuilding or navigating experience!

C'mon, folks, isn't the Lord asking too much here? We're talkin' mission impossible! It would be the equivalent of the Lord commanding you to build a space shuttle and fly you and your family to the moon.

But does any of that matter to Nephi? Nope. To him, it's simply a matter of "I will go and do."

Talk about ACTing! How many of us would have responded to this command with the same willingness and faith as Nephi did? How tempting would it have been to instead REACT with a hundred reasons why this ship building idea just ain't gonna float.

As we said before, Nephi knows what the end goal is (and it's not a life of ease and comfort on this beach). He also knows the Lord will give him all the necessary directions and assistance to get him and his family *to* that end goal.

Nephi's confidence in the Lord is expressed nicely in his quotable quote . . .

NEPHI'S QUOTABLE QUOTE

If God had commanded me to do all things I could do them. If he should command me that I should say unto this water, be thou earth, it should be earth; and if I should say it, it would be done. (1 Nephi 17:50)

And always remember, Nephi wasn't just born with this kind of faith . . . pre-programmed at birth to be the spiritual bomb diggity (like we mentioned in Chapter 1).

He has nurtured his faith, little by little, experience by experience. He caught the vision early on. He keeps that vision by using his spare time to feed his spirit. He sees the bigger picture. He lets the Lord write on his slate by "walking in the paths of righteousness." He seeks after spiritual knowledge. He chooses to ACT, instead of REACT.

All these things slowly build on each other until, as C.S. Lewis put it, Nephi's cottage has become a palace.

THAT WAS **THEN** THIS IS **NOW**

My young friend, we've been making the analogy that

Lehi & his family's journey to the Promised Land = Our journey through life toward eventual exaltation

However, there is a big difference between these two journeys:

> Lehi's was a *physical* journey, a trans**location** from one place to another.
>
> Yours and mine is a *spiritual* journey, a trans**formation** from one being to a new being in Christ.

That is the reason why Heavenly Father asks you and me to

do hard things and go through difficult experiences. He knows that it is all part of our transformation. Instead of just letting us "stay on the beach" in comfort and ease, He stretches us, tries us, challenges us, works us, shapes us, refines us, molds us into what we are destined to become —as He is.

You know what some of these growing pains are like: Feeling "out of it" socially because you won't compromise your standards. Having to change your friends for this or that reason. Dealing with tough family situations that, to say the least, are not described in any of the verses of "Love at Home." Struggling to understand certain subjects in school. Battling with your own personal weaknesses or temptations.

AND, in addition, there are several HUGE "get off the beach" experiences just around the corner for you:

—Serving a mission (especially you young men)

—Getting a job/moving out on your own

—Going to college/choosing a career path

And the biggie . . .

—Finding an eternal companion and starting a family

Basically, becoming an adult.

Yes, when you think about the "hard things" the Lord is asking of you—or *will be* asking of you in the very near future—it *can* be scary. But don't let fear paralyze you! Fear of your inadequacy? Fear of the unknown? Fear of change? Phooey! (Sorry, I couldn't think of a better word, other than "phooey.") With trust in God and with His help, you can overcome those fears and become stronger for having gone through the experience. Just like Mr. You-Know-Who, "I-Will-Go-and-Do."

Remember what the Lord told Joseph Smith in Liberty Jail as he was going through some of the hardest growing pains of his life, "All these things shall be for thy experience, and shall be for thy good" (D&C 122:7).

BY THE WAY

Skip ahead a few verses to 1 Nephi. 18:1–4. Notice how once the whole group finally buckles down and goes to work building the ship, how a different spirit seems to come over the camp. Sure, the Lord needed to give L&L a swift kick in the pants before they could get to that point (shocking the whiny-ness right out of them). But once they committed themselves to working, there is no more murmuring, no more resisting. Everyone is busy, focused on a common goal. Working.

My young friend, there's something to be said for the **power of work**. Good ol' fashioned, roll-up-your- sleeves, get-your-fingernails-dirty WORK. It's invigorating, it's satisfying, its cleansing to the spirit. Don't be afraid of work! It is becoming a lost art in today's world of technology and convenience.

SUMMING IT UP

Doctor's Report

Disease LEMUELITIS as shown by . . .
"Not Trusting that God can build you into someone better than you ever could become alone"

Symptoms - Fear of change, especially if it means doing something hard
- Content to stay right where you are

Prescription Realize that your life is a series of transformations, growing from one stage to the next. In other words . . .
Get off the beach!

Dr. Bowman
Signature

Chapter 7

We're Settin' Sail . . . "Arrrr" ya Savvy?

(Nephi's version—1 Nephi 18)

And it came to pass that we did all labor together to build Nephi's ship, and did work timbers after a very strange manner which was shown unto us by Nephi, yea, and while we were building, behold, Nephi did go into the mount oft, and did continually return unto us with more bizarre plans and ideas concerning the construction of his ship.

And after we did finish constructing the ship, behold, we did step back and take a look at the workmanship thereof, and were compelled to admit that the ship was, indeed, the bomb diggity; yea, perhaps the Lord is with us, for we know that Nephi, alone and of himself, hath no clue how to build anything (well, except for a bow).

And it came to pass that we did load the ship with all manner of provisions, yea, with fruits, and with meats, and with honey, and with many other items necessary for our survival, and we did set sail.

(What if this story were told pirate style?)

Ahoy, me hearties, we be sailin' yonder on the high seas now. Aye, it be a grand day, an' me an' me mateys be singin' an' dancin' a hornpipe with the lassies, aye, we be loaded ta the Gunwales an' makin' ourselves merry. Yo ho . . . yo ho . . . a pirate's life for me!

But Avast! That thar Nephi be spoilin' our fun once more. Arrrr! He be callin' us to repentance, tellin' us ta' "Belay that thar sauciness, me hearties!" Shiver me timberrrrs, Nephi! Its off ta' walk the plank with ya! Or perhaps we'll keelhaul ya! But alas, we be tyin' him ta that thar yardarm instead.

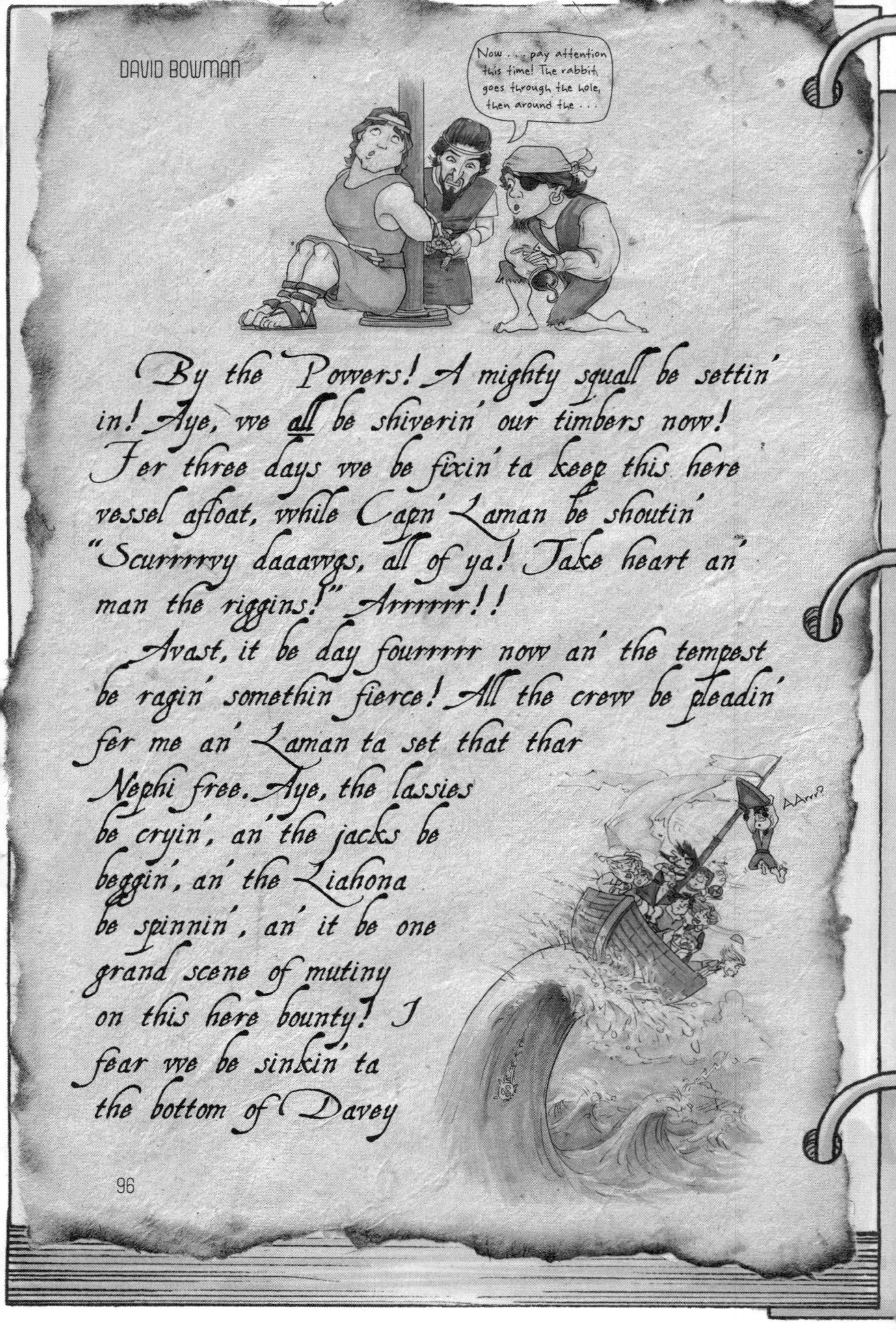

By the Powers! A mighty squall be settin' in! Aye, we *all* be shiverin' our timbers now! Fer three days we be fixin' ta keep this here vessel afloat, while Cap'n Laman be shoutin' "Scurrrrvy daaawgs, all of ya! Take heart an' man the riggins!" Arrrrrr!!

Avast, it be day fourrrrr now an' the tempest be ragin' somethin fierce! All the crew be pleadin' fer me an' Laman ta set that thar Nephi free. Aye, the lassies be cryin', an' the jacks be beggin', an' the Liahona be spinnin', an' it be one grand scene of mutiny on this here bounty! I fear we be sinkin' ta the bottom of Davey

Jones's Lockerrrrrrr . . . arrr ya savvy?

But avast, take heart, me mateys, the squall be now overrrr! Aye, fearin' that we be goin' ta that thar Fiddler's Green 'n the sky, we be smartly untyin' that scallywag, Nephi. He be prayin' an' the good Lord be stoppin' the storm. Aye, what be up with that thar lily-livered, Lord-lubber Nephi, anyway? It seems the good Lord be always listenin' ta him an' blessin' him. Oh well, at least the black spot be takin' off **our** heads now. Arrr!

And after many days of mannin' the riggins, an' hoistin' the sails, an' swabbin' the decks, an' navigatin' by that thar Liahona, I be perched atop the yardarm one day, when suddenly . . . "Well, I'll be a bucaneerin' bilge rat . . .

Land ho, me hearties!"

WHAT'S **REALLY** HAPPENING HERE

Ever since the family left Jerusalem, Nephi has proven himself again and again to be the spiritual leader. Nephi knows it. Lehi knows it. The Lord knows it. And Laman and Lemuel can't stand it! They see Nephi *not* as the Lord's mouthpiece, but only as a threat to their authority as the oldest brothers. It's a total pride thing.

See, in ancient custom, it was the right of the firstborn to rule the household (that would be Laman). However, the firstborn could give up that right to rule due to his poor choices (again, that would be Laman). In which case, another brother would be chosen to rule in his place (and that would be Nephi).

That is why anytime Nephi offers correction, instruction, or counsel to his brothers (such as "Belay that thar sauciness, me hearties" or, translated from Pirate into English, "Hey, brothers, quit partying!"), all they can think is one thing: "We will not that our younger brother shall be a ruler over us" (1 Nephi 18:10). They are completely stuck in a one-track mind-set, like a broken record repeating itself over and over in their heads. It doesn't matter what the correction or counsel is. They just hate the fact that it's coming from Nephi.

Pride.

"**KNEW NOT** THE DEALINGS OF THAT GOD WHO HAD CREATED THEM"

L&L didn't understand that sometimes the Lord works through other people to get a message to you. It could be counsel from your parents, extended family members, Church leaders, the general authorities, an inspired friend . . . perhaps even from a younger brother. The trick is to become humble enough to receive those messages, even if it means needing to change something about yourself.

THAT WAS **THEN** THIS IS **NOW**

How do you respond to someone correcting you? For people infected with Lemuelitis, it ain't pretty. For them, it's all about (once again) pride. Ego. Power struggles. Getting offended. Getting defensive. Retaliation. REACTing.

My young friend, you are in the phase of your life's journey where you crave **autonomy.** Oooh, there's a good vocab word for ya: autonomy. It means *"independence, freedom, ability to be one's own master."* Autonomy is a good thing because it motivates you to make those needed steps toward becoming an adult (like we talked about in the last chapter).

But don't get so caught up in your autonomy that you can't handle instruction or advice. Stay humble. Learn from those who have walked the road before you. Your journey toward eternal life requires it.

In my years teaching seminary, I've had a few youth who came into my class claiming to "not be into the Church thing." As I got to know them, I realized that the reason for their rebellious streak was actually a power struggle with their parents. They felt like their parents "pushed" the Church on them way too much, so they resisted.

However, I quickly learned that it had nothing to do with the Church. As a matter of fact, they actually enjoyed my seminary class and felt the Spirit there. Deep down, they knew the gospel was true. But they were afraid of showing it because that would be like admitting to their parents that they (their parents) were right all along. In other words, they let the **source** of the counsel (their parents) get in the way of their accepting the **content** of their counsel (to live the gospel).

How sad! How stinky! Smells like Lemuelitis to me.

Besides not being able to take correction, L&L have also, once again, lost all perspective of the bigger picture (surprise, surprise!).

See if you can detect the flaws in their way of thinking:

So, Laman & Lemuel, it's been smooth sailing so far out on the big blue. You're feelin' pretty good. The sea-faring life suits you just fine. Well then, hey, by all means . . . throw a deck party! Have some fun! Break open the kegs, me hearties, and get "exceedingly rude"! Why not? You deserve it!

Forget the fact that it's <u>the Lord</u> who gave you the designs to build the very ship you are partying on. Forget the fact that you're out the middle of the blasted ocean and it's <u>the Lord</u> who is steering you and keeping you afloat at this very moment. Forget the fact that you are completely, 100% at the mercies of the Lord. Forget the fact that what you're doing is offensive in His sight . . . and that <u>the Lord</u> could sink you at any given second if He so desired!

Do you see the short-sightedness of their vision? For L&L, it's always about the here and now. What feels good at the moment. Nothing more than that. And if anybody tries to put a damper on their fun (like Nephi) by reminding them of what they *should* be doing and the consequences of their actions, they only respond with anger!

In other words, they think only of themselves, not realizing that what they do affects the fate of the entire ship-bound group. Yeuuck! So Lemuel!

HOW 'BOUT THAT **NEPHI**

Once again, Nephi is "Da Man" in this story. As they set sail, he humbly keeps the vision of where they are going and by whose power they are being led there. He speaks up "with much soberness" when something needs to be said to his partying shipmates. He patiently endures four days of being tied up on the deck of a storm-tossed ship. After finally being untied (with wrists and ankles "swollen exceedingly"), Nephi gets the Liahona working again. He humbly prays away the storm. Nothing ruffles him. And he humbly uses the Liahona to eventually guide the ship to the Promised Land.

Humbly, humbly, humbly. See the difference as compared to L&L's pride?

And what was the key to Nephi's humility? See if you can find it in his Quotable Quote:

NEPHI'S QUOTABLE QUOTE

Nevertheless, I did look unto my God, and I did praise Him all the day long; and I did not murmur against the Lord because of mine afflictions. (1 Nephi 18:16)

What more can we say? You go Nephi! 😊 Thanks for showing us a better way.

BY THE WAY

Why didn't Nephi go see the pirate movie?
Because it was rated "Arrrr." 😊

SUMMING IT UP

Doctor's Report

Disease LEMUELITIS as shown by . . . "Pride"

Symptoms
- Power struggles (especially with parents)
- Not being able to take correction
- Thinking only of yourself and what you want, regardless of how it affects others

Prescription "Look to God and Praise *Him* all day long" (WHY? Because who can possibly toot their own horn and think they're all that . . . when they are praising the Almighty GOD and HIS infinite power??? Yeah . . . kinda puts things in perspective.)

Dr. Bowman

Signature

Chapter 8

"Awake! And be Men!" (Yeah, Dad, whatever)

(Nephi's version—2 Nephi 1; 4:12–13; 5:1–7, 20–21)

And it came to pass our ship did finally arrive in the Promised Land, and I did recommend we name it "Treasuuurrrre Island" but alas, we have to name it what Nephi wants to, yea even "The Promised Land" (yea, an exceedingly original name ☺ . . . not! ☹).

And behold, we did pitch out tents, and Laman did exhort me to pitch my tent off a cliff, for behold, eight years usage and another year rolled up in the ship and he saith that my tent doth now stink exceedingly, yea, and others say it stinketh with an exceedingly great stink; but behold, to me, it doth not stink. Nevertheless, it mattereth not what I thinketh, for my wife saith it stinketh, and thus my tent is given the ol' heaveth-hoeth according to her words. And thus endeth the days of the tent of Lemuel.

And we did start planting seeds of every kind, and did find all manner of wild beasts in the forests, and all manner of gold and silver, insomuch that I did call the land "Treasuuurrrre Island" anyway. Arrrr! ☺

And it came to pass that my father, Lehi, did wax exceedingly old, being stricken in years; yea, even his gray hairs were about to be brought down to lie low in the dust, from whence no traveler can return (I did copy those last lines from Nephi's record, for behold, they soundeth cool).

Wherefore, Lehi did call his family together to give each of us one last nagging before he croaketh (uuuhh, those words I did not copy).

And it came to pass that our father, Lehi, did go off for the space of many hours about how this land was a special land, a blessed land, yea, a land where people get led to an' stuff, a land where you hafta serve God or bad stuff happens, wherefore, this land is your land, this land is my land, from Irreantum, to the Treasure Island, YADDA YADDA YADDATH.

And behold, I did fall into another deep sleep at this point, yea, my dad's long-windedness having this effect on me.

When suddenly I did **AWAKE** from my slumber, for someone did shout **"AWAKE!"** Yea, even Lehi did cry **"AWAKE!"**, therefore I did **AWAKE!**

And he did cry unto me,

AWAKE from a deep sleep! (Yup, Dad, I'm awake now. Thanks.)

Yea, even from the sleep of hell (Nope, it was actually a rather nice sleep.)

And shake off the awful chains by which ye are bound (Uh . . . what chains?)

AWAKE! And arise from the dust (OKAY, I <u>*WAS*</u> LYING IN THE DIRT. MY BAD, BUT . . .)

and be MEN! (HEEEY, NOW THAT WAS LOW.)

AWAKE, my sons (YEEES! I'M AWAKE ALREADY!)

Put on the armor of righteousness (UH, ARMOR? HUH? WAIT A MINUTE . . . OH, I SEE . . .)

AND IT CAME TO PASS THAT I, LEMUEL, DID PROMPTLY DISCERN THAT MY FATHER WAS SPEAKING TO US . . . *METAPHORICALLY* (OOHH).

BUT BEHOLD, MY FATHER DID ALSO SPEAK WORDS THAT WERE GRIEVOUS TO BE BORN, YEA, EVEN REGARDING NEPHI, AND HOW WONDERFUL HE IS, AND HOW WE SHOULD NOT BE SO MEAN TO HIM, AND HOW WE ARE ALL SUPPOSED TO LISTEN TO HIM, AND DO WHAT NEPHI SAYS, AND THAT NEPHI

is in charge because the power of God is with him, and that Nephi is all that and a bag of unleavened chips. Nephi, Nephi, Nephi!

And I beheld steam steaming forth from Laman's ears.

Nevertheless, our father did continue to RAMBLE ON for the space of many hours, and after he had made an end of speaking, behold, he did die (well, not right away . . . I mean, he eventually died). And thus we see the end of him who perverteth the ways of reason and logic by taking his family away from their inheritance in Jerusalem all those years ago.

And it came to pass that not many days after father's death, know-it-all Nephi did commence to try to boss everyone around (for the thousandth time), according to the multitude

OF HIS TRICKY TACTICS, INSOMUCH THAT LAMAN AND I DECIDED IT WAS EXPEDIENT THAT NEPHI HAVE A LITTLE ACCIDENT. HEH HEH HEH.

AND AS WE WENT FORTH TO ASSIST NEPHI IN SPENDING SOME "ONE ON ONE TIME" WITH HIS FATHER, BEHOLD, WE WERE EXCEEDINGLY ASTONISHED TO FIND THAT NEPHI, AND HIS FAMILY, AND ALL THOSE WHO FOLLOWED NEPHI **HAD DISAPPEARED**, YEA, THEY FLEWETH THE COOP, RANNETH AWAY, EVEN GOT THEMSELVES HENCE.

AND NOW, BEHOLD, FOR THE FIRST TIME SINCE WE LEFT THE LAND OF OUR INHERITANCE, WE ARE FINALLY RID OF LEHI **AND** NEPHI, AND MY JOY DOTH EXCEED ALL JOYNESS! FOR NOW WE ARE **FREE**! YEA, WE ARE **FREE** TO FOLLOW WHATEVER LAMAN DOTH TELL US TO DO, YEA, **FREE** TO BE CUT OFF FROM THE PRESENCE OF THE LORD, YEA, **FREE** TO BE SLAVES TO OUR APPETITES, YEA, EVEN **FREE** TO WEAR LOIN CLOTHES AND GET EXCEEDINGLY TAN. AAAHH . . . **FREE**, ALAS . . . **FREE**, ALAS!

AND I, LEMUEL, DO MAKE AN END OF WRITING FOR A SEASON, FOR BEHOLD, MY FAVORITE TV SHOW *ANCIENT AMERICAN IDLE* DOTH START SOON, AND I HAVE MUCH MISCHIEF AND SUBTLETY TO ACCOMPLISH BEFORE THEN, THEREFORE, I MAKE AN END.

And we did live after the manner of Lemuelitis-ness.

WHAT'S **REALLY** HAPPENING HERE

Okay, L&L, ya dimwits, this is it. Your *last* chance to step up and (as Lehi puts it) be **MEN**!

You have just arrived in the Promised Land. (See, it DOES exist! Lehi and Nephi were right all along.) It's beautiful. It's the perfect place to settle and start a new civilization. It's *also* the perfect place to put aside your anger and frustrations, spanned over years of hard wilderness survival, and start over.

In other words, it's a time of "new beginnings" (yes, even though you're not young women, you can have them too ☺). You have wives and children who are looking to you for righteous leadership. You *can* put off the natural man, through the Atonement of Christ, and become who you were always intended to be. You can change.

Furthermore, your parents are on their deathbeds. Your entire lives they have taught you, encouraged you, begged you even to follow the Lord and keep his commandments. Your blessed father is attempting one last time to get through your thick skulls and hardened hearts, pleading with you to repent. It's his dying wish.

So . . . (drum roll please) . . . with all that said . . . Laman & Lemuel . . . **what-are-you-going-to-do???**

DUDE! DON'T BE A LEMUEL

Sigh. And yet once again . . . Lemon & Lamo BONK! They don't change one bit! Dude, will they ever stop being so Lemuel?? I guess not.

What amazes me is not just that L&L bonk, but also how quickly they bonk! How instantly they forget the pleadings of their father and turn right back to their old destructive thought patterns:

"And it came to pass that not many days after his death, Laman and Lemuel and the sons of Ishmael were angry with me because of the admonitions of the Lord." (2 Nephi 4:12–13)

And then they whine (read it with your best whiney voice):

"Our younger brother thinks to rule over us; and we have had much trial because of him; wherefore, now let us slay him, that we may not be afflicted more because of his words. For behold, **we will not have him to be our ruler; for it belongs to us, who are the elder brethren, to rule over this people**." (2 Nephi 5:3)

Fortunately, the Lord warns Nephi of his brothers' murderous intentions. Nephi takes his family and all the believers with him, and they flee into the wilderness. And thus begins the permanent separation of the Lamanites and the Nephites.

In describing his brothers, Nephi made this interesting comment about their final condition:

"[L&L] had hardened their hearts against [the Lord], that they had become like unto a flint." (2 Nephi 5:21)

Flint is an extremely hard form of quartz. When struck against steel, it can create a spark. Sounds like L&L, doesn't it? Completely hardened to the spirit and only good for creating sparks of anger.

> By age, Laman and Lemuel were men, but in terms of character and spiritual maturity they were still as children. They murmured and complained if asked to do anything hard. They didn't accept anyone's authority to correct them. They didn't value spiritual things. They easily resorted to violence, and they were good at playing the victim.
>
> (Elder D. Todd Christofferson, "Let Us Be Men," *Ensign*, Nov. 2006)

So, in the end, Laman & Lemuel basically succeed in one thing: **stooping to entirely new levels of pathetic-ness.** Way to go, guys! Lemuelitis has completely eroded your spiritual senses. You are officially beyond being cured!

HOW 'BOUT THAT **LEHI**

I love Lehi's final father's interview with his wayward sons (2 Nephi 1:13–29). Read it, it's powerful. You can just feel this Dad's love for his boys, his intense desire for them to be the men their Father in Heaven knows they can be. From day one to his dying breath, Lehi does not give up on them . . . parents never do.

How 'bout those parents of *yours*? Sometimes you might feel they are getting on *your* case. But always remember, they love you like no other person in this world does. And that kind of love won't just keep quiet if they see you going in a wayward direction.

So, love 'em right back! Listen to them. Do what they ask you to do. Be humble and teachable. Make 'em happy by the choices you make. You owe it to them. You owe everything to them.

LEHI'S QUOTABLE QUOTE

But behold, the Lord hath redeemed my soul from hell; I have beheld his glory, and I am encircled about eternally in the arms of his love. (2 Nephi 1:15)

I hope to be able to say the same thing at the end of my life.

"**KNEW NOT** THE DEALINGS OF THAT GOD WHO HAD CREATED THEM"

Throughout this book, we've been talking about all the ways L&L "knew not the dealing of that God who had created them." This lack of understanding about their Father in Heaven hurt them spiritually. But it was their apathy toward the *greatest* of all "the dealings of that God who had created them" that killed them spiritually.

Lehi saw it in his vision:

"And Laman and Lemuel partook not of the fruit, said my father." (1 Nephi 8:35)

They never felt the love of God. They never grasped the love of their Savior, nor felt the joy His cleansing power brings. And without partaking of that divine love, L&L had no love to give. No love for their parents, no love for their siblings, no love for anybody. They were simply cold, empty, loveless souls. And all of their anger, their murmurings, their rebellions, and even their fears, were mere by-products of their loveless hearts.

Compare that with Nephi. As mentioned in chapter 4, he experiences this love for himself and his life is never the same. He lets it transform every part of him, until his soul "delighteth in the things of the Lord" (2 Nephi 4:16). Father Lehi describes how he was "encircled about eternally in the arms of His love." And I'm sure Sariah would have plenty to say about the love of Jesus Christ, as would Sam.

Partaking of the fruit (savoring the love of God) is really what life is all about.

And it's the same today.

THAT WAS **THEN** THIS IS **NOW**

"And this is life eternal, that they might know thee the only true God, and Jesus Christ, whom thou hast sent." (John 17:3)

Your journey to your "Promised Land" (eternal life) is all about how well you come to know the love of your Heavenly Father and Jesus Christ. How much you are filled with Their love . . . that's what matters! So, make pleasing Them your first priority, and watch your life become extraordinary. And at your journey's end, you will find yourself back in Their presence. You will have become as They are. And you will be greeted with the words, "Well done, thou good and faithful servant."

SUMMING IT UP

Doctor's Report

Disease FULL-BLOWN LEMUELITIS

as shown by . . .

"Becoming Hardened (like unto Flint)"

(Continuous exposure to Lemuelitis leads to this dreaded final condition)

Symptoms - Not being able to feel the Holy Ghost anymore

- Having no love in your heart
- Cut off from the presence of God

Prescription Eat plenty of fruit! (Make sure it's the love of God variety ☺)

Dr. Bowman

Signature

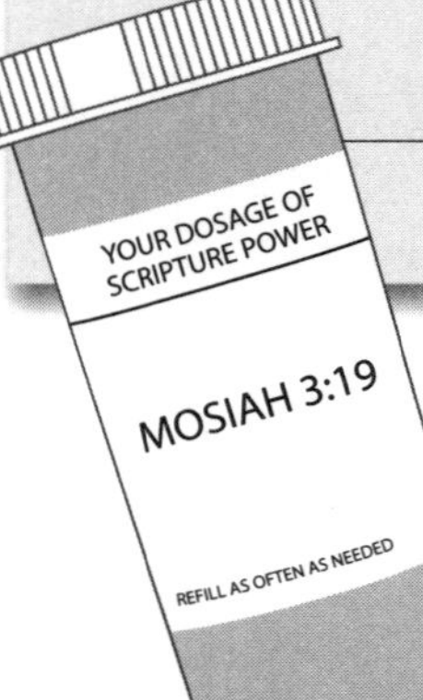

WRAPPING IT ALL UP . . .

Well, my friend, we've come to the end of our journey. You've learned all about Lemuelitis straight from Mr. Lemuel himself. Nasty disease, isn't it? AND you've learned how to conquer the disease by following Nephi's example. Let's recap our doctor's reports, shall we?

Remember . . . LEMUELITIS starts rearing its **ugly head** when you . . .

1) Know not the dealings of that God who has created you

Prescription—Catch the vision & see the BIGGER picture

2) Lack faith that you can do "hard things" that the Lord commands

Prescription—Take six Nephibuprofen stones and call me in the morning

3) Gospel fence ride

Prescription—Keep your vision by using your free time to feed your spirit

4) Make no effort to seek out spiritual knowledge for yourself

Prescription—Make that EXTRA effort in your search for spiritual knowledge

5) REACT, instead of ACT

Prescription—ACT by getting the spirit of Christ in your heart

6) Don't trust that God can build you into something better than you ever could become alone

Prescription—Get off the beach by accepting that your life is a series of transformations

7) Show Pride

Prescription—Look to God and Praise Him all day long

And finally, in its full-blown stage . . .

8) Become Hardened (like unto Flint)

Prescription—Eat plenty of fruit! (Make sure it's the Love of God variety ☺)

What else have you noticed about Lemuelitis? Sum it up time . . .

As we said in the beginning, people infected with the disease are still capable of doing good things. Like L&L. They obey the commandments . . . sometimes. They "humble themselves before the Lord" . . . sometimes. They pray and give thanks . . . sometimes. They feel bad for their mistakes and do better . . . sometimes.

But are they consistent? No. Do any of these "righteous" actions have a lasting effect on their character . . . on who they really are inside? Not so much. They go through some of the motions, but don't allow themselves to be changed inside. They never really put their hearts into it. As a matter of fact, the only times that

L&L do any "good" is when something drastic happens to them or when they are afraid for their lives. That's why folks infected with Lemuelitis are still capable of **doing** good . . . but have a hard time **becoming** good.

> The Final Judgment is not just an evaluation of a sum total of good and evil acts—what we have done. It is an acknowledgment of the final effect of our acts and thoughts—what we have become. It is not enough for anyone just to go through the motions.
>
> (Elder Dallin H. Oaks, "The Challenge to Become," *Ensign*, Nov. 2000)

Resisting Lemuelitis and becoming a Nephi is really all about your attitude. Your motives. Your desires. And it's about consistency. It's about what's happening to your heart *on the inside* . . . while you are consistently making good choices *on the outside.*

Now can you see why Lemuelitis is so common today (even among this righteous generation of LDS youth)? It's the easier way to go. It's the default setting. In other words, you automatically get the disease unless you're actively striving to follow Christ. You can't just "slide by" in the Church, putting forth minimal effort, without contracting Lemuelitis. Scary, huh?

King Benjamin described the disease AND the cure *perfectly* in this scripture mastery:

> For the natural man [Lemuelitis] is an enemy to God, and has been from the fall of Adam, and will be, forever and ever, unless he yields to the enticings of the Holy Spirit, and putteth off the natural man and becometh a saint through the atonement of Christ the Lord, and becometh as a child [or as a Nephi], submissive, meek, humble, patient, full of love, willing to submit to all things which the Lord seeth fit to inflict upon him, even as a child doth submit to his father. (Mosiah 3:19)

Oh, and one more thing . . . Why do you think I focused this book on Lemuel instead of Laman? We usually think of Laman as the initiator of all the murmurings and rebellions, with Lemuel just going along with his older brother. So, why not call this book *Dude! Don't be a Laman* since he's the one who seems to start all the problems?

Well, that's just my point. For every Leading Laman out there, there are fifty Lemming Lemuel's who just "go with the flow." They are much more common. Lemuels don't stand strong for the right, so instead, they naturally gravitate toward their baser instincts and become followers. In other words, I see **Laman**itis as actively rebelling against God (LDS youth aren't like that). I see **Lemuel**itis as passively giving into the natural man inside of you. Hmm, much more subtle and tempting. *That's* what LDS youth (all of us, for that matter) have to contend with.

May Father in Heaven bless you, my young friend! You are good! You are striving to do what's right, otherwise you wouldn't be reading this book. Kudos! You're on the right track. Dealing with the natural man (Lemuelitis) is as much a part of your life here on Earth as breathing. So, don't get discouraged. The reward is worth it. Keep following the prescriptions Nephi and the other prophets set for you! Catch the vision. Eat the good fruit (the love of God) as often as you can. And then let God's love ooze out of you so that others can feel His love by knowing you. Our Lemuelitis infected world needs that now more than ever.

And when Lemuelitis tries to creep its way into your veins (as it always does) just shout to yourself:

"DUDE! Don't be a Lemuel!

ABOUT THE AUTHOR/ILLUSTRATOR

Following his service as a full-time missionary in the Philippines, David Bowman graduated with a degree in Illustration from Brigham Young University. He has since served as a release-time seminary instructor as well as a counselor and speaker at numerous EFY conferences.

David's special love is making the gospel come to life for young people. For children, he is the author/illustrator of the best-selling *Who's Your Hero?* and *Firmly Founded* series. For pre-teens and teens, his book *What Would the Founding Fathers Think? A Young Americans Guide to Understanding What Makes Our Nation Great & How We've Strayed* is also a must read! He and his wife, Natalie, and their five children live in Arizona.

David Bowman has also produced several fine art paintings depicting the Savior. His artwork (along with all his books) can be found at **www.davidbowmanart.com**